Cambridge Primary

Hodder Cambridge Primary
Maths

Learner's Book

Stage 3

Josh Lury

Series editors: Mike Askew
and Paul Broadbent

HODDER
EDUCATION
AN HACHETTE UK COMPANY

Author acknowledgements

With warm thanks to Jackie Mace for her help in shaping and developing this title.

The Publisher is extremely grateful to the following schools for their comments and feedback during the development of this series:
Avalon Heights World Private School, Ajman
The Oxford School, Dubai
Al Amana Private School, Sharjah
British International School, Ajman
Wesgreen International School, Sharjah
As Seeb International School, Al Khoud.

Photo acknowledgements

We would like to thank the following for their permission to reproduce photographs:
p.26 © Look Die Bildagentur der Fotografen GmbH/Alamy Stock Photo; **p.46** *bt*, **p.88** *tr* (**both**) © Bogdan Ionescu/123rf; **p.46** *bl*, **p.88** *tl* (**both**) © Daniel Buus/123rf; **p.46** *br* © Tatiana Popova/123rf; **p.49** *tl* © Pixphoto/123rf; **p.49** *tc* © Hongqi Zhang/123rf; **p.49** *cl* © Vassiliy Prikhodko/123rf; **p.49** *c* © Tykhyi/123rf; **p.49** *bl* © Eric Isselee/123rf; **p.49** *tr* © Hecke/123rf; **p.49** *cr* © Bon Appetit/Shutterstock; **p.49** *br* © Wannee Nimcharoen/123rf; **p.53** © Blend Images/Alamy Stock Photo; **p.84** *l* © Greg Notzelman/123rf; **p.84** *c* © Ron Bull/Alamy Stock Photo; **p.84** *cr* © Vito Arcomano/Alamy Stock Photo; **p.84** *br* © Danny Hooks/123rf; **p.129** © Potapova Valeriya/123rf

t = top, *b* = bottom, *l* = left, *r* = right, *c* = centre

Practice test exam-style questions are written by the author.

Whilst every effort has been made to carefully check the instructions for practical work described in this book, schools should conduct their own risk assessments in accordance with local health and safety requirements.

Every effort has been made to trace all copyright holders, but if any have been inadvertently overlooked the Publishers will be pleased to make the necessary arrangements at the first opportunity.

Hachette UK's policy is to use papers that are natural, renewable and recyclable products and made from wood grown in sustainable forests. The logging and manufacturing processes are expected to conform to the environmental regulations of the country of origin.

Orders: please contact Bookpoint Ltd, 130 Milton Park, Abingdon, Oxon OX14 4SB. Telephone: (44) 01235 827720. Fax: (44) 01235 400454. Lines are open from 9.00–5.00, Monday to Saturday, with a 24 hour message answering service. You can also order through our website www.hoddereducation.com

© Josh Lury 2017

Published by Hodder Education

An Hachette UK Company

Carmelite House, 50 Victoria Embankment, London EC4Y 0DZ

Impression number 6

Year   2021 2020

Cover illustration © Steve Evans

Illustrations by Alex van Houwelingen, Vian Oelofsen, Rose Elphick and Steve Evans

Typeset in FS Albert 15/17 by DTP Impressions

Printed in Slovenia

A catalogue record for this title is available from the British Library

9781471884368

Contents

I am Felix.

I am Irina.

Introduction

Explore the picture or problem.

What do you see? What can you find out?

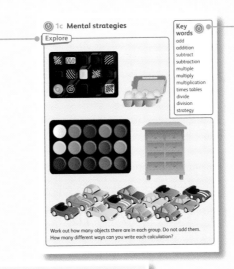

Key words are in a list for you to learn.

Learn new maths skills with your teacher. Look at the diagrams to help you.

Practise the maths you have learnt. Write any answers in your exercise book.

Read these hints and tips to help you **think like a mathematician**.

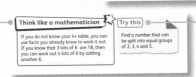

Try this challenge activity to make you think carefully about the maths.

At the end of each unit try the **Self-check** activities. What have you learnt?

1a Counting and numbers to 1000

Key words
count on
count back
pattern
number line
rule
increase
decrease
output
function

Explore

1	2	3	4	5	6	7	8	9	10
11	12	13	14	15	16	17	18	19	20
21	22	23	24	25	26	27	28	29	★
31	32	33	34	35	36	37	38	39	40
41	42	43	44	45	46	47	48	49	★
51	52	53	54	55	56	57	58	59	★
★	62	63	★	65	★	67	★	69	70
71	72	73	74	75	76	77	78	79	80
81	82	83	84	85	86	87	88	89	★
91	92	93	94	95	96	97	98	99	100

What helps you to work out the hidden numbers?

Counting on and back

Learn

What are the missing numbers?

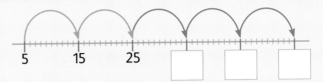

5   15   25

What numbers are missing from this pattern?

| 105 | 115 | 125 | | | |

This number track looks the same as the number line.

Work out how much you need to add on each time.

Practise

1 Work out the missing numbers.

a
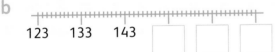
23   33   43

b
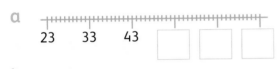
123   133   143

c
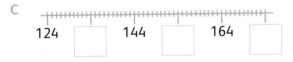
124   [ ]   144   [ ]   164   [ ]

d
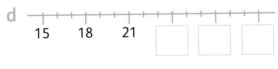
15   18   21

e
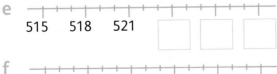
515   518   521

f
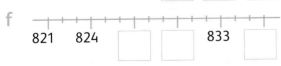
821   824   [ ]   [ ]   833   [ ]

2 Copy and complete.

a

| 40 | 35 | 30 | | |

b

| 41 | 36 | 31 | | |

c

| 142 | | 132 | | 122 | |

d

| 242 | | 252 | | 262 | |

e
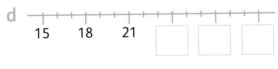
| | | 45 | 55 | |

f

| 45 | | | | 55 |

3 Copy and complete these patterns.
The first one has been done for you.

a (42) 52 (62) 72 82 92

b (42) (47) 52 57 ( ) ( )

c (92) [ ] (88) [ ] (84) [ ]

d ( ) 92 [ ] 84 ( ) 76

e 42 [ ] ( ) [ ] ( ) 67

Try this

Design your own circle and square pattern.
Follow these rules.

- The number 10 must be in a circle.
- The number 100 must also be in a circle.

Can you design more than three different patterns that follow these rules?

Function machines

Learn

1 What happens when these numbers are INPUT into machine A?

0 10
5 20
100

Input

A
+10

2 What information do you need to work out the function?

5 0 10
20
100

Input

B
?

Practise

1 Work out the OUTPUTS for each machine.

INPUTS
14
24
25
124
125
136

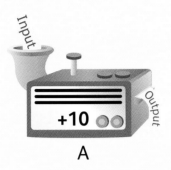

A

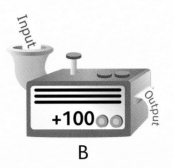

B

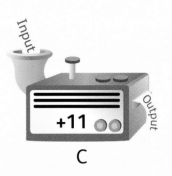

C

2 Work out the INPUTS for each machine.

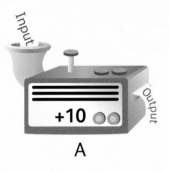

A

B

C

OUTPUTS
114
124
125
224
325
536

3 What are the FUNCTIONS of these machines?

Inputs
30
50
80

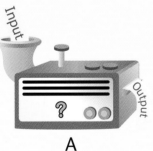

A

Outputs
60
80
110

Inputs
198
297
496

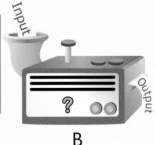

B

Outputs
203
302
501

Inputs
203
302
901

C

Outputs
199
298
897

Try this

A '+11' and a '−6' function machine are joined together. Choose five inputs for the joined machine. What is the output for each input? What do you notice?

1b Number and place value

Explore

Key words

number line
place value
hundreds
tens
ones
estimate
more
less

Imran

Yee Lung

Serina

Lee

Joshua

Makemba

100 m
Finish

Estimate how far each learner has run.
How can you make your estimates more correct?

Three-digit numbers

Learn

1 Where should these numbers go on the number line?

90 60 50 25 99 10

What does the mark in the middle represent? How do you know?

```
0                                                    100
```

2 Where should these numbers go on this number line?

300 700 250 850 401 501

Work out what each little mark represents.

```
0                                                    1000
```

Practise

1 These number lines are marked in tens. What numbers should replace the letters? The first one in **a** has been done for you.

a
```
        a     b  c      d      e  f
0      20
```

b
```
          a      b  c      d      e  f
100
```

2 These number lines are marked in tens. Replace the letters with numbers.

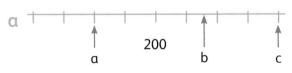

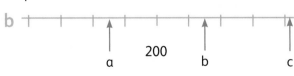

a
```
            200
      a         b         c
```

b
```
            200
      a         b         c
```

3 Write an odd and an even number that could go in each shaded section.

a

300   400

b

500   600

11

10 or 100 more and less

Learn

The number 345 has been broken down into its hundreds, tens and ones.

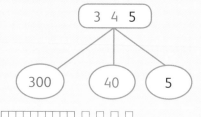

Breaking a number into smaller parts is called partitioning.

1 You can use partitioning to work out 100 more than 345.

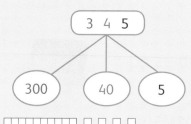

$345 + 100 = 445$

2 You can also use partitioning to work out 10 less than 345.

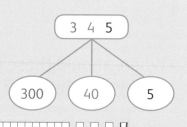

$345 - 10 = 335$

Practise

1 a Copy the partioning diagrams.
Use them to work out 100 more
and 100 less.

b Work out 10 more and 10 less.

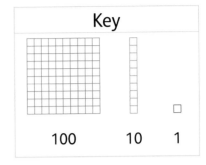

Key

100   10   1

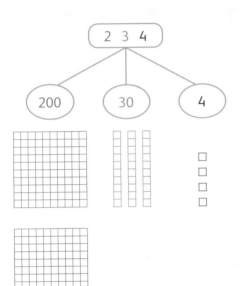

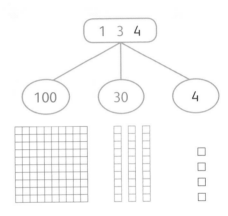

2 Draw your own partitioning diagram to show the number 432.

a Find 100 more and 100 less.

b Find 10 more and 10 less.

Think like a mathematician

Think carefully about place value.
The digit '3' in 432 does not actually stand
for 3. It stands for 30, because it is in the
tens position. What does the '4' stand for?

3 Work out the missing numbers.

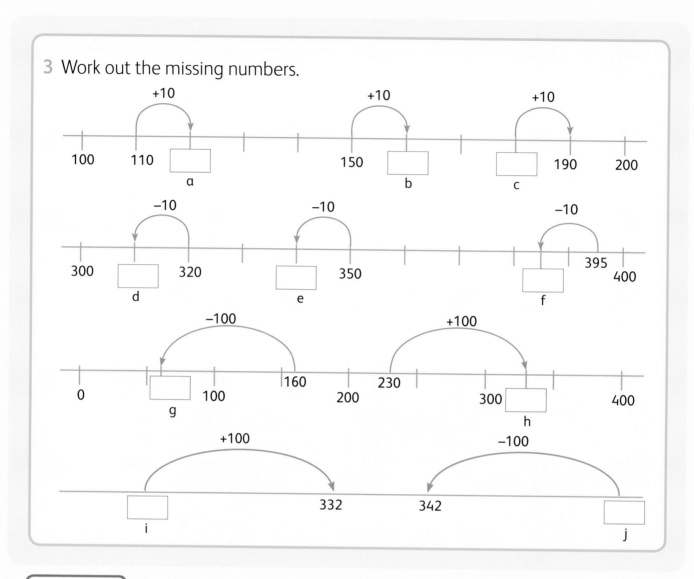

Try this

I am thinking of a number. I add 10 to my number and get 142. What is my number?

I am thinking of a number. I add 100 to my number and get 642. What is my number?

I am thinking of a number. I add 10 to my number, then I take away 100 from the answer. I get 142. What is my number?

⟳ 1c Mental strategies

Explore

Key words

add
addition
subtract
subtraction
multiple
multiply
multiplication
times tables
divide
division
strategy

Work out how many objects there are in each group. Do not add them.
How many different ways can you write each calculation?

Multiplication and division facts

Learn

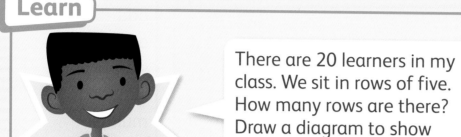

There are 20 learners in my class. We sit in rows of five. How many rows are there? Draw a diagram to show how you worked it out.

I can write this calculation as a multiplication fact and as a division fact.
$20 \div 5 = 4$
$4 \times 5 = 20$

Think like a mathematician

If you do not know your 4× table, you can use facts you already know to work it out. If you know that 3 lots of 6 are 18, then you can work out 4 lots of 6 by adding another 6.

Try this

Find a number that can be split into equal groups of 2, 3, 4 and 5.

Practise

1 How many learners in each class?

   a Class A has five rows of 3.

   b Class B has three rows of 5.

   c Class C has four rows of 5.

   d Class D has five rows of 4.

   e Class E has six rows of 2.

   f Class F has two rows of 7.

2 How many rows of 5 in each class?

   a Class 1 has 15 learners.

   b Class 2 has 30 learners.

   c Class 3 has 45 learners.

   d Class 4 has 55 learners.

   e Class 5 has 60 learners.

   f Draw a diagram for each classroom.

   g Write a multiplication and a division fact for each classroom.

3 A class of 24 learners visits the park. The learners are split into groups of equal size. How many learners are there in each group if there are:

   a two groups?   b three groups?   c four groups?

   d six groups?   e 12 groups?

Try this

A class of 36 learners visits the park. Answer 3a–e for this class.

Addition and subtraction pairs to 20

Learn

Each card has a calculation on the front, and its answer on the back.

1 What is on the back of these cards?

| 5+4 | 5+6 | 7+5 |

2 Write five different additions and subtractions for the front of each card.

| = 16 | = 17 | = 18 |

Practise

1 Answer these.

a 3 + 7	13 + 7	12 + 7	b 4 + 6	14 + 6	13 + 6
c 5 + 5	5 + 15	4 + 15	d 5 + 8	5 + 9	6 + 9
e 4 + 7	5 + 6	6 + 5	f 8 + 8	7 + 7	6 + 6

2 Match each addition with a subtraction that gives the same answer.

| 5 + 3 | 4 + 7 | 8 + 7 | 3 + 9 | 3 + 2 | 11 + 7 |
| 13 − 5 | 14 − 9 | 19 − 7 | 15 − 0 | 20 − 2 | 17 − 6 |

3 Write down five different additions and subtractions that could be on the front of each card.

| = 7 | = 17 | = 11 |

Try this

Find at least five different ways to work out each of these answers.

$$\boxed{} + \boxed{} - \boxed{} = 5$$

$$\boxed{} + \boxed{} - \boxed{} = 15$$

$$\boxed{} - \boxed{} + \boxed{} - \boxed{} = 10$$

Addition pairs to 100 and 1000

Learn

☐ + 300 = 1000

7 + 3 = 10

70 + 30 = 100

700 + 300 = 1000

You can use patterns to solve this calculation.

I think this calculation is 25 + 85, because 20 add 80 is 100.

25 + ☐ = 100

That is a mistake many people make. Can you see why it is wrong?

Practise

1 Answer these.

a   4 + 6 = ☐
40 + 60 = ☐
400 + 600 = ☐

b   10 = 1 + ☐
100 = 10 + ☐
1000 = 100 + ☐

c   10 − ☐ = 3
100 − ☐ = 3
1000 − ☐ = 3

d   2 + 8 = ☐
20 + 80 = ☐
200 + 800 = ☐

e   10 = ☐ + 5
100 = ☐ + 50
1000 = ☐ + 500

f   8 = 10 − ☐
80 = ☐ − 20
☐ = 1000 − 200

2 How big is each jump? The first one has been done for you.

a

d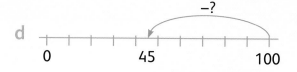

b

e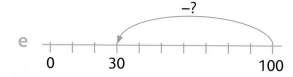

c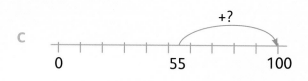

f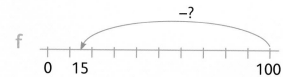

3 Answer these.

a 2 + ☐ = 10

2 + ☐ = 11

20 + ☐ = 100

20 + ☐ = 101

200 + ☐ = 1000

200 + ☐ = 1001

b 3 + ☐ = 10

3 + ☐ = 20

30 + ☐ = 100

30 + ☐ = 200

300 + ☐ = 1000

300 + ☐ = 2000

c 100 − ☐ = 45

101 − ☐ = 45

101 − ☐ = 35

101 − ☐ = 36

☐ − 85 = 16

☐ − 85 = 14

Try this

Use your mental strategies for adding and subtracting to solve these.

a 250 + ☐ = 1000   b 450 + ☐ = 1000

c 1000 − 750 = ☐   d 1000 − ☐ = 150

Self-check

A Counting and numbers to 1000

1 What numbers are missing on this number line?

359 ☐ 379 ☐ 399 ☐

2 Copy and complete this pattern. Did you count on or back?

☐ 94 90 ☐ ☐ 78

3 What is the FUNCTION of this machine?

Inputs
267
541
808

Outputs
367
641
908

B Numbers and place value

1 Use the partitioning method to break down 458 into hundreds, tens and ones.

2 Write the place value of the underlined numbers.
   a 10<u>3</u>   b <u>5</u>61   c 9<u>8</u>7

3 Write the numbers that are 10 less and 100 more than 643.

C Mental strategies

1 There are 30 bean plants planted in rows of five in the vegetable garden. Draw a diagram to show how many rows of beans there are in total.

2 Write a multiplication fact and a division fact for the calculation from question 1.

3 Write three additions and three subtractions to make a total of 20 each time.

4 Answer these.
   a 40 + ☐ = 100   b ☐ + 250 = 1000

⏻ 2a 2-D shapes

Explore

How many squares?

Look for different-sized squares, not just the obvious ones.

Key words
triangle
quadrilateral
square
rectangle
properties
right angle
symmetry
symmetrical

Can you see any rectangles? What is the same and what is different about squares and rectangles?

Properties of 2-D shapes

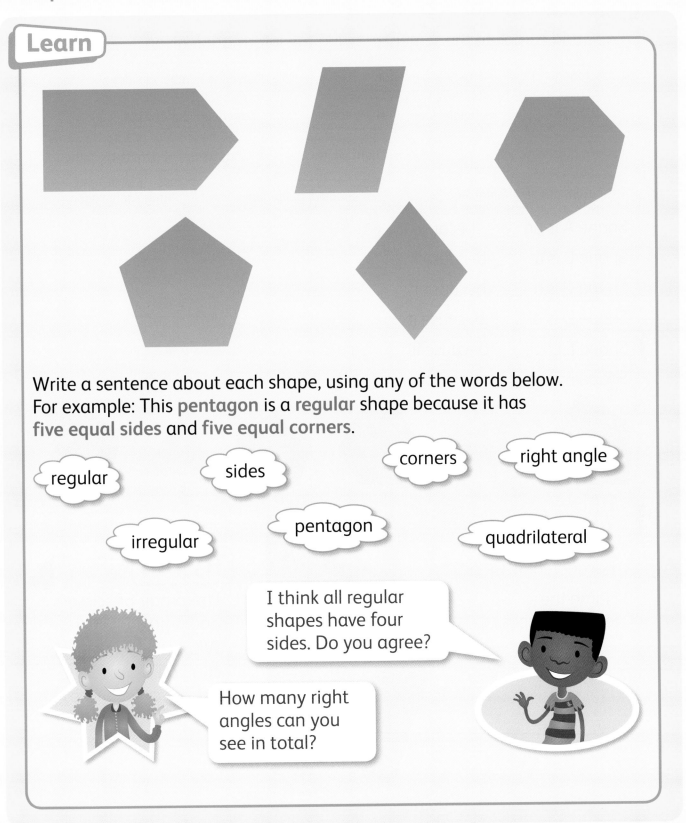

Learn

Write a sentence about each shape, using any of the words below.
For example: This **pentagon** is a **regular** shape because it has
five equal sides and **five equal corners**.

corners

right angle

regular

sides

irregular

pentagon

quadrilateral

I think all regular
shapes have four
sides. Do you agree?

How many right
angles can you
see in total?

Practise

1 Copy and complete the sentences using the information given.

| octagon | | regular pentagon | | has double the number of sides of a kite |

| triangle | | rectangle | has 3 corners | has equal sides and equal angles |

| regular hexagon | has 4 right angles | has 6 sides of different lengths |

| has 5 sides of different lengths | irregular pentagon | irregular hexagon |

Shape A is an _____ because it _____.

Shape B is a _____ because it _____.

Shape C is a _____ because it _____.

Shape D is a _____ because it _____.

Shape E is a _____ because it _____.

Shape F is an _____ because it _____.

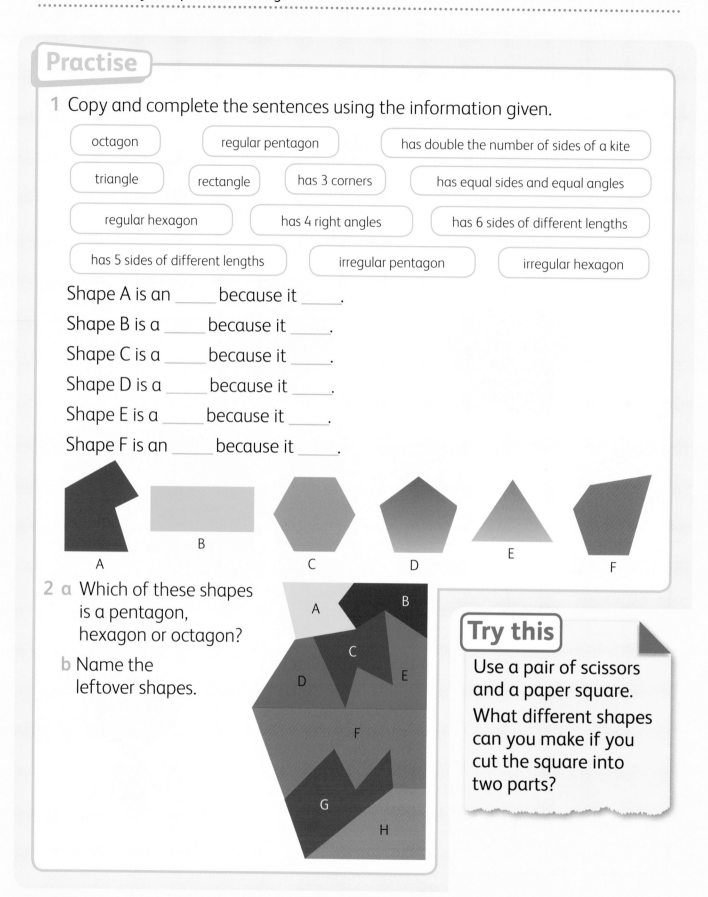

A   B   C   D   E   F

2 a Which of these shapes
     is a pentagon,
     hexagon or octagon?

   b Name the
      leftover shapes.

Try this

Use a pair of scissors
and a paper square.
What different shapes
can you make if you
cut the square into
two parts?

Symmetrical shapes

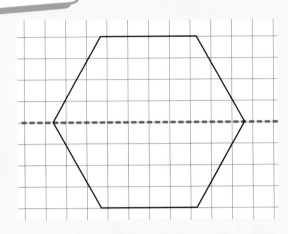

Can you see any other lines of symmetry?

How many lines of symmetry do you think there are in total?

Try this

Draw a shape that has more than one line of symmetry. For an extra challenge, see if you can draw a shape that has three lines of symmetry.

Practise

1 a List the quadrilaterals that have line symmetry.

  b Name the shapes with more than one line of symmetry.

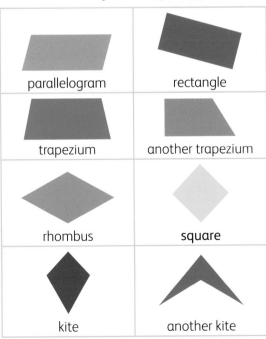

parallelogram	rectangle
trapezium	another trapezium
rhombus	square
kite	another kite

2 Draw these symmetrical shapes, showing all the lines of symmetry.

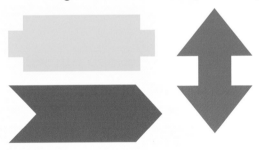

3 Use 12 cubes to make a symmetrical shape, then draw it.

4 Use 10 cubes. Make five different symmetrical shapes.

5 Use cubes to make a shape with four lines of symmetry. How many right angles does your shape have?

2-D shapes in the environment

Learn

What different 2-D shapes can you see in this photograph?

List all the shapes with right angles.

Are there any symmetrical shapes? How do you know?

Practise

1 List all the shapes you can see in the photograph above. Use three headings:

   a Odd number of sides

   b Has a right angle

   c Has curved sides.

2 Look around your classroom or school building.

   List five shapes that:

   a have a right angle

   b are symmetrical

   c have no right angles.

   Draw a diagram of each shape.

Try this

Draw a map of your classroom, or your whole school. Which different shapes do you need to draw?

Write estimated measurements for the lengths and widths of the main parts of your map.

2b 3-D shapes

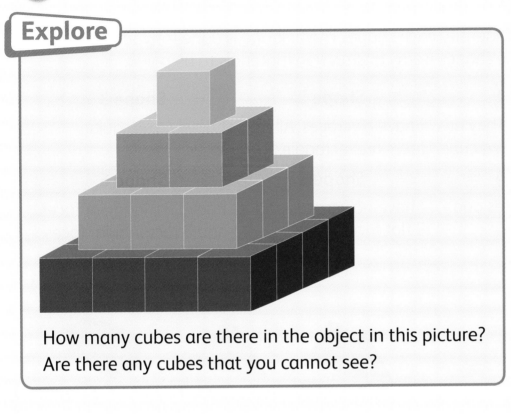

How many cubes are there in the object in this picture?
Are there any cubes that you cannot see?

Key words

vertex
vertices
face
edge
cube
cuboid
pyramid
prism
base
triangular

Properties of 3-D shapes

Learn

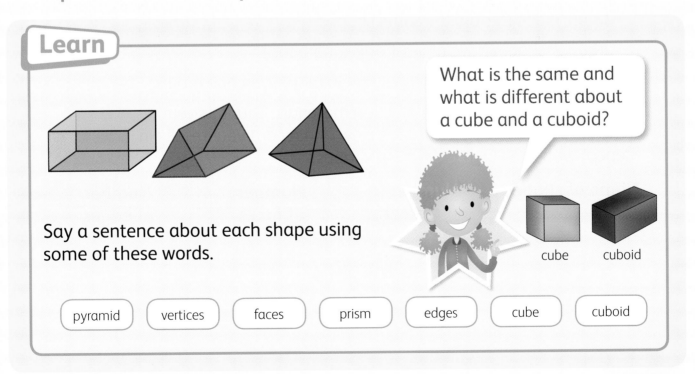

What is the same and what is different about a cube and a cuboid?

cube   cuboid

Say a sentence about each shape using some of these words.

pyramid   vertices   faces   prism   edges   cube   cuboid

Practise

1   Use the clues to identify each shape. The first one is done for you.
    Find or make the shapes from construction materials to help you.

Shape 1	Shape 2	Shape 3
I have 6 faces. They are all squares. I am a cube.	I have 8 vertices. All my faces are rectangles.	I have 4 triangular faces.
Shape 4	**Shape 5**	**Shape 6**
I have no vertices and no edges.	I have no vertices and 2 flat faces.	I have 2 triangular faces and 3 rectangular faces.

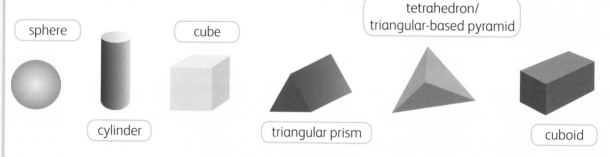

sphere   cube   tetrahedron/ triangular-based pyramid

cylinder   triangular prism   cuboid

2 a Sort the shapes from question 1 into these groups.

      Group 1: all faces are the same shape.

      Group 2: shapes have at least one square face.

   b Are there any shapes that could go in more than one group?

3 Make a 3-D shape from construction materials. Count its vertices,
   faces and edges. Copy the table below and record your results in it.
   Repeat with five or more different shapes.

Name of shape	Number of vertices	Number of faces	Number of edges

Nets of 3-D shapes

Learn

How are these two pictures related?

What is the object on the right called?

Try this

Make a pyramid and a prism out of construction materials. Take them apart and then draw a net for each.

Practise

1 Use this table to match the clues to the shapes.

Clue	How many triangular faces?	How many square faces?	How many rectangular faces?
Clue 1	0	6	0
Clue 2	2	0	3
Clue 3	4	1	0
Clue 4	0	2	4

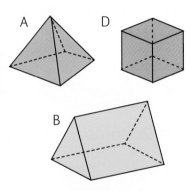

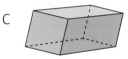

2 Copy these nets. Predict which nets will fold up to make a cube. Then make all the objects.

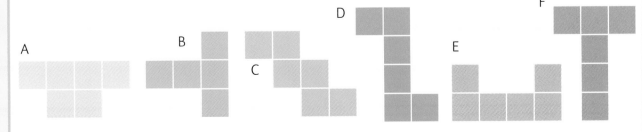

3 There are many different nets that make a cube. Draw eight or more.

Self-check

A 2-D shapes

Look at the shapes and answer the questions.

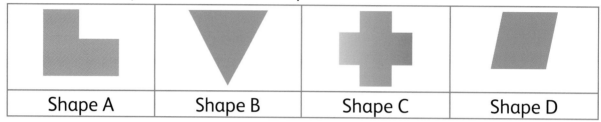

| Shape A | Shape B | Shape C | Shape D |

1 What is the same and what is different about Shapes A and D?

2 How many sides and right angles does each shape have?

3 Copy and complete the sentence.
Shape B is a ___ because it has ___. It has ___ lines of symmetry.

B 3-D shapes

1 Name the shape. How many faces does it have?

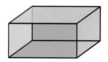

2 Name the shape. How many edges and vertices does it have?

3 What shape does the net below make?

(⟳) 3a Addition and subtraction

Key words (⟳)

addition
add
sum
total
subtraction
subtract
take away
minus
inverse

Explore

1 How much do the different animals weigh?

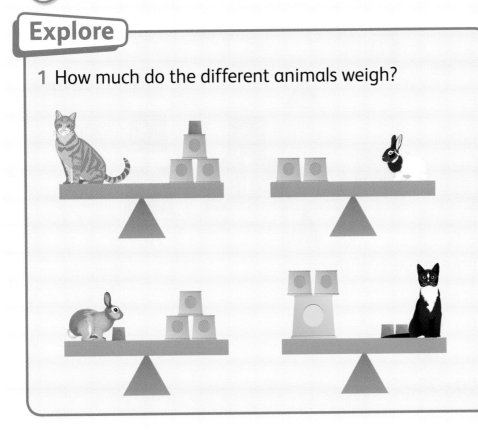

Key	
▮	1 kg
▯	2 kg
▢	5 kg

Equal values

Learn

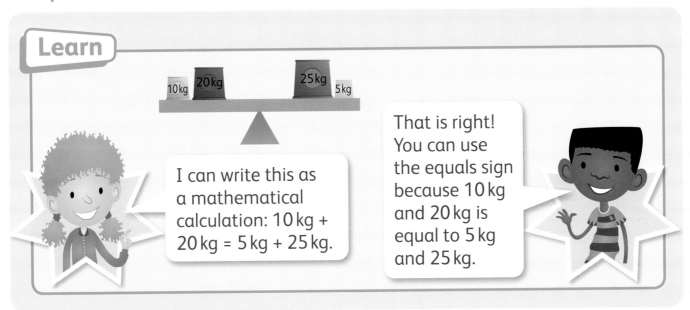

I can write this as a mathematical calculation: 10 kg + 20 kg = 5 kg + 25 kg.

That is right! You can use the equals sign because 10 kg and 20 kg is equal to 5 kg and 25 kg.

Practise

1 Write these as mathematical calculations.

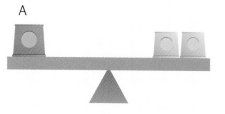

Key	
	25 kg
	50 kg
	100 kg
	200 kg
	500 kg

2 Draw a balance diagram for each of these.

   a 200 = 100 + 100

   b 250 = 50 + 50 + 50 + 100

   c 100 + 50 = 25 + 25 + 100

   d 200 + 25 = 50 + 100 + 25 + 50

3 Copy and complete.

   a 55 + ☐ = 100
      55 + ☐ = 100 + 5
      55 + ☐ = 100 + 25
      55 + ☐ = 200 + 25

   b ☐ + 56 = 100
      ☐ + 56 = 100 + 20
      ☐ + 56 = 100 + 50
      ☐ + 56 = 200 + 50

   c 56 + 50 = 100 + ☐
      66 + 60 = 100 + ☐
      76 + 70 = 100 + ☐
      86 + 80 = 99 + ☐

Try this

How many different solutions can you write for this?

20 − ☐ = ☐ + 10

Checking using the inverse

Learn

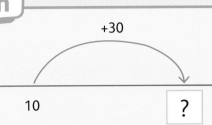

+30

10   ?

−30

?   40

What is the same and what is different about these number lines?

I think that addition and subtraction are inverse operations.

The second number line is an inverse of the first.

Try this

31 − 20 − 10 = 1
51 − 10 − 20 = 11
71 − 10 − 30 − 20 = 21
81 − 30 − 10 − 5 − 5 = 31

These calculations need more than one inverse step to check them.

Use the inverses of each subtraction. Which are incorrect?

Practise

1 Draw a number line to solve each addition. Then, draw a second number line to show the inverse operation.

a 12 + 30 = ☐   b 50 + 12 = ☐

   22 + 30 = ☐   40 + 22 = ☐

   32 + 30 = ☐   30 + 32 = ☐

2 Check these by doing the inverse operation. Show your working out.

a 52 − 20 = 32   b 62 − 30 = 32
c 92 − 50 = 32   d 51 − 20 = 31
e 61 − 20 = 51   f 91 − 50 = 51

Write the correct calculations.

Adding three or more numbers

Learn

These are the scores in a quiz.

	Team A	Team B	Team C
Round 1	11	15	21
Round 2	20	5	12
Round 3	9	19	9

Which team won? How did you work it out?

Practise

1 Add these spinner scores. Order the numbers to make the additions quicker to perform.
Write your calculations.

a

b

c

d

e

2 Work out how much you will pay for:

a a pencil, a ruler and a paintbrush

b a sharpener, an eraser and a pen

c a pencil, a pen and a paintbrush

d a paintbrush, a sharpener and a pencil.

Show your calculations.

Stationery price list for
a stationery shop

Pencil .... 30 cents

Pen.............................. 70 cents

Eraser......................... 20 cents

Paintbrush............... 60 cents

Ruler........................... 20 cents

Sharpener................ 40 cents

3 Oli visits the stationery shop. He has 200 cents. Can he buy four items?

Try this

Write a price list for six items for your own shop. Your partner chooses three items to buy. Choose the best order to add the prices together.

⟳ 3b Multiplication and division

Explore

There are enough cakes for each leaner to have two.

There are some adult helpers.

Every learner and every adult can have two sandwiches.

How many adult helpers are there?

Key words ⟳

double
half
halve
multiply
divide
place value
digit
partition

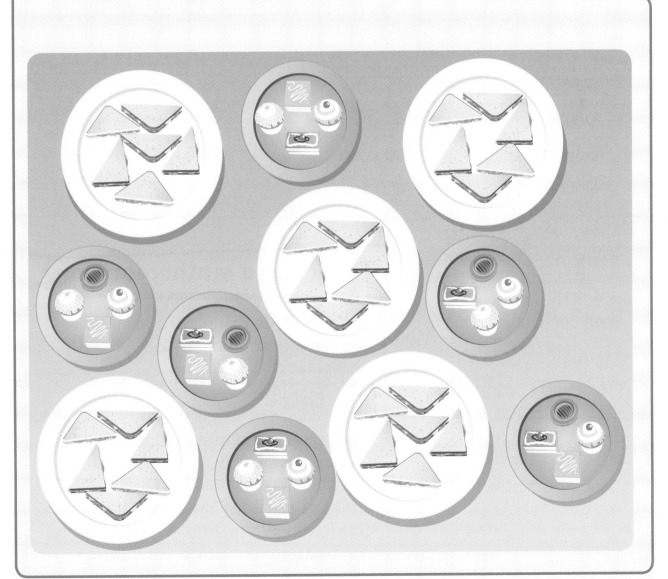

Doubling by partitioning

Learn

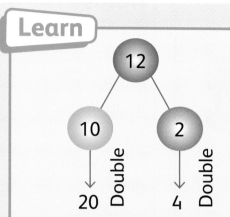

Double

Double

Double 12

When doubling a number, you can break it down (partition it) to make it easier.

Practise

1 Answer these.

a Double 3 = [ ]

Double 30 = [ ]

Double 300 = [ ]

b 4 × 2 = [ ]

40 × 2 = [ ]

400 × 2 = [ ]

c Double 14 = [ ]

Double 16 = [ ]

Double 18 = [ ]

2 Make sure these football teams have enough boots. How many boots do they need? The first one has been done for you.

Team A – 11 players

There are 11 players and each player has two boots.
11 × 2 = 22 boots

Team B – 13 players

Team C – 17 players

Team D – 19 players

Think like a mathematician

Remember, doubling is the same as multiplying a number by 2.

Try this

Four sports teams need socks. The Red team has 15 players, the Yellow team has 13 players, the Blue team has nine players and the Green team has 16 players. Find the total number of socks in two different ways.

Halving by partitioning

Learn

These diagrams show two ways to find half of a number.

What is the same and what is different about each method?

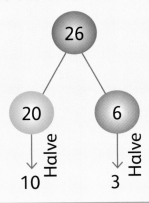

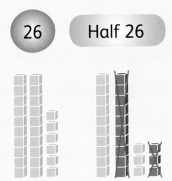

Practise

I think of a number, double it and then say the answer.

1 Work out Irina's starting numbers.

a 14   b 24   c 44   d 64

e 104   f 204   g 404

2 Answer these.

a Half of 20 = ☐

Half of 40 = ☐

Half of 60 = ☐

Half of 80 = ☐

Half of 100 = ☐

b Half of 200 = ☐

Half of 400 = ☐

Half of 600 = ☐

Half of 800 = ☐

Half of 1000 = ☐

c Half of ☐ = 11

Half of ☐ = 22

Half of ☐ = 33

Half of ☐ = 44

Half of ☐ = 55

Describe the patterns you see in your answers.

Halving trickier numbers

Learn

I am finding it tricky to find half of 74. I know half of 4, but what is half of 70?

Explain how to find half of 70.

Is there more than one way?

Practise

1 Draw diagrams to show these.

a Half of 30

b Half of 50

c Half of 70

d Half of 90

2 What is half of each of these?

a		b		c	
300		32		330	
500		54		550	
700		76		770	
900		98		990	

Try this

Keep halving each number until you end up with an odd number.

Which number can be halved the most?

800	500	300
440	540	450

Multiplying by 10

Learn

A

100s	10s	1s
	1	7

B

100s	10s	1s
	7	1

C

100s	10s	1s
1	7	0

D

100s	10s	1s
7	1	0

What do you see in these diagrams? What is the same and what is different about each diagram?

Try this

Can you find more than five different answers to this calculation?

 × 10 = 100 −

Remember that '=' means 'is equal to'.

Practise

1 Draw a place value chart to show each number after it has been multiplied by 10.

a

100s	10s	1s
	1	3

b

100s	10s	1s
	2	3

c

100s	10s	1s
	5	3

d

100s	10s	1s
	9	3

e

100s	10s	1s
	3	1

f

100s	10s	1s
	3	5

g

100s	10s	1s
	3	2

h

100s	10s	1s
	3	9

2 Work out the missing numbers in each list.

a 21 × 10 = ☐
   31 × 10 = ☐
   41 × 10 = ☐

b 10 × 45 = ☐
   10 × 55 = ☐
   10 × 65 = ☐

c ☐ × 10 = 990
   ☐ × 10 = 880
   ☐ × 10 = 770

How far can you continue each list?

3c Calculation problems

Explore

Why do you think this is called a magic square?

2	7	6
9	5	1
4	3	8

I love puzzles!

What is your starting point for completing this magic square?

	9	
	5	
8	1	

Where do we start?

You can also make a magic square using these numbers.

10	20	30	40	50	60	70	80	90

If you are really confident, try using these numbers.

2	4	6	8	10	12	14	16	18

strategy
method
diagram
number story
array

Arithmagon

Learn

This kind of puzzle is called an arithmagon. You can work out the number in a square by adding the numbers in the circles it is joined to.

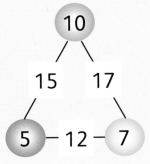

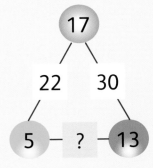

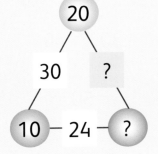

Look at the numbers in the circles. Look at the numbers in the squares. Work out the missing numbers.

Practise

1 Copy and solve these.

a
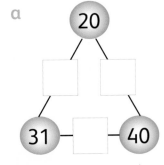

b
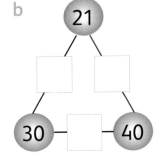

c
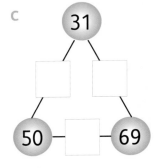

2 Copy and solve these.

a
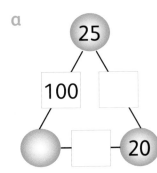

b
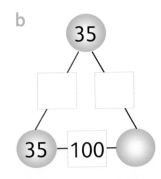

c
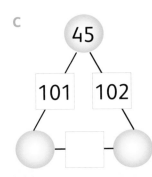

Try this

These puzzles are trickier than they look. See if you can work out the missing numbers. You might make a few mistakes before you find the right answer.

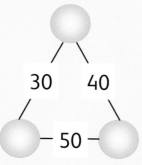 30   40   — 50 —

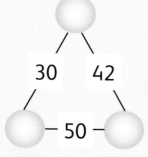 30   42   — 50 —

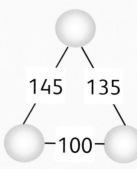 145   135   —100—

Think like a mathematician

'Trial and improve' is a method for solving problems. When you think of your first idea, try it to see if it works. If you are close, then you just need to change your idea a bit. If you are not close, then you will need to change your idea a lot.

Drawing pictures to solve word problems

Learn

The question says: 'There are 10 goats and 10 ducks in a field. How many legs are there altogether?'

I know how to solve problems like this! I always draw a simple picture to help me.

Would you draw the animals as you would in an art lesson?

Practise

Draw pictures for each of these word problems. Then answer the questions. The first one has been done for you.

1 An octopus and a starfish are in a tank. How many tentacles are there altogether?

> An octopus has eight tentacles.
> A starfish has five tentacles.
> 8 + 5 = 13

2 There are ten octopuses and ten starfish in a tank.

  a How many tentacles are there altogether?

  b If you needed to buy socks for the tentacles of the octopuses, how many pairs would you need?

  c How many tentacles are there if one octopus and one starfish are left in the tank?

3 Tao bought 3 boxes of sweets for $4 per box. Afia bought four bags of sweets for $3 per bag.

  a They had $15 dollars each. Was that enough?

  b How much did they spend altogether?

  c If they combined their change, could they buy any more bags or boxes of sweets?

4 Oli's tree is twice as tall as Eleni's tree. Eleni's tree is twice as tall as Marie's tree. Marie's tree is 4 m tall.

  a How tall is each person's tree?

  b How much taller is the tallest tree than the shortest tree?

  c If you chopped each tree in half, how tall would it be? What if you chopped them in half again?

Try this

Make up your own word problem to go with these calculations.

25 + 100

5 × 5

double 75

Explaining your methods

$$10 + 20 + 30 + 40 + 50$$

How would you solve this addition?

How many different methods can you think of?

Explaining your methods and comparing them is one of the best ways to learn.

1 The number on the front of each bus shows how many people are in it.

How many people came to visit the zoo?

WELCOME TO THE ZOO

20 30 60 10 70 50

Think of two different ways to do the calculation.

Discuss this with your partner. Then each of you try a different method.

Compare your results at the end.

2 How can you use these arrays to help you work out these?

$5 \times 4 = 20$
$6 \times 4 =$

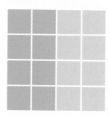

$2 \times 4 = 8$
$4 \times 4 =$

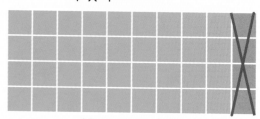

$10 \times 4 = 40$
$9 \times 4 =$

Self-check

A Addition and subtraction

1 Write the missing numbers to make the calculation equal.

☐ + 150 = ☐ + 90

2 Do the calculation. Then write the inverse.

71 – 40 = ☐

3 These are the number of learners in each Stage 3 class of our school.

| Class A: 25 | Class B: 22 | Class C: 19 | Class D: 28 | Class E: 30 |

How many learners are there in Classes B, E and D altogether?
Show how you worked this out.

B Multiplication and division

1 Use partitioning to double and halve the number 32.

2 Multiply 18 x 10. How many hundreds, tens and ones are in the answer?

3 Write this calculation in two different ways. The answers must be the same.

4 × ☐ = 32 and ☐ × ☐ = 32

C Calculation problems

1 Write two different ways to solve this addition.
20 + 20 + 10 + 50 + 100

2 Draw pictures to solve this problem. Then write a calculation to show how you worked out the answer.

There are six red pencils and six green pencils on each desk in the classroom. How many pencils will there be on four desks?

3 Make up your own problem to go with this calculation.

Double 150

Unit 4 Measure and problem solving

4a Money

Explore

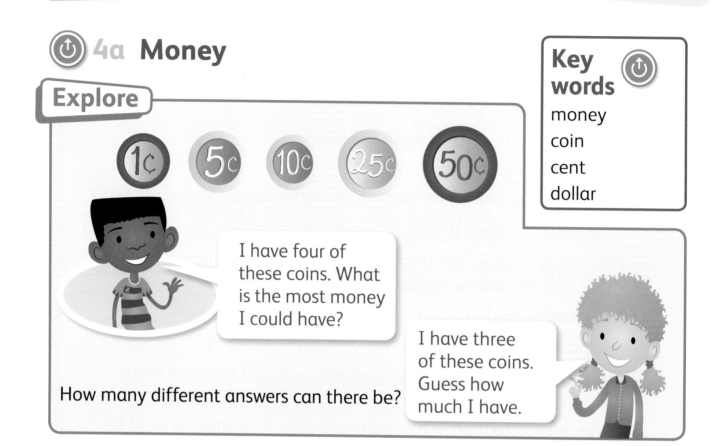

I have four of these coins. What is the most money I could have?

I have three of these coins. Guess how much I have.

How many different answers can there be?

Key words

money
coin
cent
dollar

Paying for items

Learn

You have some of each kind of coin.

1¢ 5¢ 10¢
25¢ 50¢

Can you think of more than one way to pay for each item?

$1.50

90¢

75¢

Practise

1 Choose four different notes from those given above. What are all the different amounts you can make?

2 Write down three different ways to pay for each piece of fruit. Select from the coins above.

Fruit price list	
apple	30c
banana	40c
orange	50c
mango	70c

Think like a mathematician

When you are looking for lots of different answers, it is a good idea to use a list. A list helps you to be systematic.

Try this

- Make a price list for a toy shop. Mum wants to buy five different toys. She has only $20. What can she buy?

- Make a price list for four different meals at a cafe. Dad wants to buy four meals for the family. He has only $15. What does he buy?

Working out change

Learn

Think of three different solutions to this.

$$? + ? = \boxed{\$ \; 5 \; \$}$$

I want a ball that costs $3. I give you $5, you give me the ball and $2, because …

 + $2 = $5

Try this

Make up a word problem to go with these money calculations.

- Start with $5, leave $3 change.
- Start with $10, leave $3 change.
- Start with $10, leave $3 change, buy two items.
- Start with $10, leave $3 change, buy four items.
- Start with $10, leave $2 change, buy four items that cost the same.

Practise

1 How much change do you get from $10 for each item?

2 Franco bought two items and paid with a $20 note. What did he buy if he got:

   a $6 change?

   b $8 change?

   c $7 change?

   d $11 change?

Clothes sale price list

Hat.....................$7

Coat..................$9

Gloves..............$5

T-shirt...............$4

Trousers......$6.50

Jumper.......$5.50

4b **Length**

Explore

Key words ⟳

estimate
measure
centimetre
metre
kilometre
scale
units
length
height

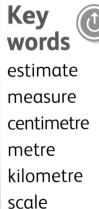

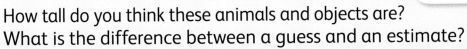

How tall do you think these animals and objects are?
What is the difference between a guess and an estimate?

Reading scales

Learn

You can also use a tape measure and a ruler to measure accurately.

If you do not have a tape measure, use strips of paper that will fold and twist. Then measure the strips of paper using a ruler.

Practise

1 Use a tape measure and be as accurate as you can.
   Take these measurements and record them:

   a width of your palm   b from your elbow to your middle fingertip

   c length of your foot   d around your wrist

   e from the back of your knee to your heel

   f length of your longest finger.

2 Which items are twice as long as another?

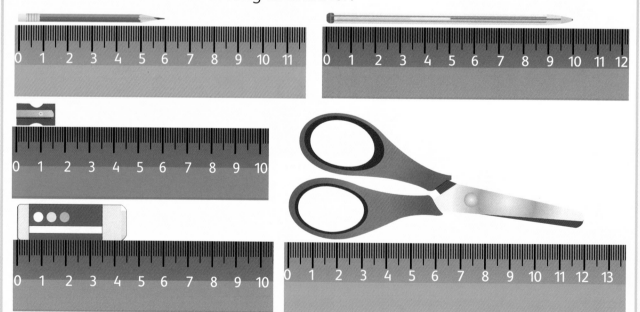

3 Estimate the length of two different items that fit on your desk.
Measure them.
Compare your estimates with your measurements.
Choose three more items and make new estimates.
Measure to check if your estimates are improving.

Decide what
you need to do
to improve your
estimates.

Record your results in a table like this.

Object	Estimate	Actual measurement
Sharpener	7 cm	
Eraser	4 cm	

Try this

Use two different ways
to work out the length
of the pencil sharpener.

Metres and kilometres

Learn

All the different measure words can be confusing.

What is the same and what is different about centimetres, metres and kilometres?

Practise

1 Copy the two columns. Then join the matching pairs. The first one has been done for you.

200 cm	1 km
300 cm	1 m
3 000 m	2 km
2 000 m	3 km
50 cm + 50 cm	3 m
500 m + 500 m	2 m

2 Think of something that is:

1 km away	2000 m away
200 cm away	5 km away
5 m away	1000 km away
1000 m away	500 m away
500 cm away	

Discuss your answers with a partner.

Try this

Draw a map to show how you get to school. Add measurements to show how long each part of the journey is. Use metres and kilometres.

Think like a mathematician

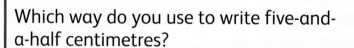

Which way do you use to write five-and-a-half centimetres?

5.5 cm $5\frac{1}{2}$ cm

52

⏻ 4c Time

Explore

What clues tell you the time in this picture?

What would you add to the picture to give more clues about the time of day or when in the year this is?

Key words ⏻

second

minute

hour

time

half past

quarter past

quarter to

Units of time

Learn

Give good estimates of how long these activities take.

Why might different people take different amounts of time to do these?

Describe the same time in two different ways.

Ⓐ

Ⓑ

Ⓒ

Ⓓ

Practise

1 Match these activities with a sensible estimate of how long they take.

Activity	Estimates
A Maths lesson	one hour
Eating an apple	90 minutes
A film	2 minutes 30 seconds
Playtime	two hours
A song	15 minutes
Going shopping	three minutes
Running 100 metres	20 seconds

2 Copy and complete these. The first one has been done for you.

   a one minute = 60 seconds

   b two minutes = _____ seconds

   c ten minutes = _____ seconds

   d 11 minutes = _____ seconds

   e one hour = _____ minutes

   f two hours = _____ minutes

   g ten hours = _____ minutes

   h 11 hours = _____ minutes

3 Use your answers to question 2 to help you to answer these. The first one has been done for you.

   a How many seconds in four minutes?

   There are 60 seconds in one minute. So there will be 240 seconds in four minutes.
   $60 \times 4 = 240$

   b How many minutes in nine hours?

   c How many hours is 300 minutes?

   d Which is longer: 180 seconds or five minutes?

   e Which is longer: 240 minutes or three hours?

Try this

$30 + 30 = 60$

$10 + 10 + 10 + 10 + 10 + 10 = 60$

How many more repeated additions can you find that make 60?

Telling the time

Learn

What do these numbers show?

Try this

Write a timetable of events that happen in a normal day.
Include: I wake up at _____.
I go to school at _____.
I eat dinner at _____.

Practise

1 How many minutes have passed the hour?

2 What will the time be in 5 minutes?

3 Order these clocks from earliest to latest. Write the letter that goes with each clock. If you get it right, the letters will spell a word.

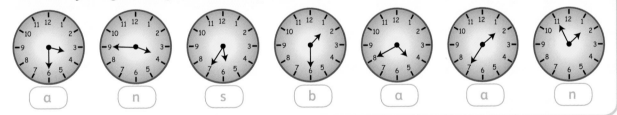

a   n   s   b   a   a   n

Think like a mathematician

Remember how the minutes go up in fives, like the five times table.

Self-check

A Money

1 How much change do you get if you pay with these notes and coins?

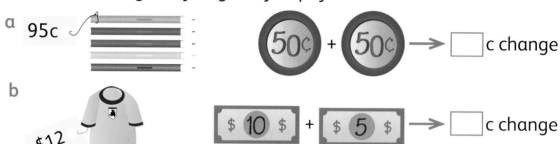

a 95c

☐ c change

b $12

☐ c change

B Measuring length

1 Estimate the length of your pencil. Now measure it. How accurately did you estimate?

2 Copy and complete the sentences.

There are ☐ cm in 1 m and ☐ m in 1 km. So, there will be 500 cm in ☐ m and 3 000 m in ☐ km.

3 Read the length of this pencil in centimetres. What would the length of a pencil twice as long as this one be?

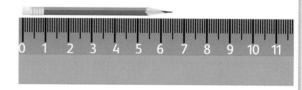

C Time

1 Match the times in the first row with the times in the second row.

| 10 minutes | 60 seconds | 5 hours | 240 minutes | 9 hours | 90 seconds |

| 540 minutes | 600 seconds | 1 minute 30 seconds | 4 hours | 1 minute | 300 minutes |

2 Copy the clock face. Draw the hands on the clock to show five minutes before half past eight.

3 Write a sensible amount of time it takes to do these things.

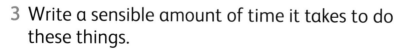

a Wash your hands   b Watch a TV programme   c Make a sandwich

Unit 5 Problem solving and review

5a Problem solving

Explore

12.30

Half price
after 4.30 p.m

1 m deep

2 m deep

1   2   3   4   5   6

The problems in this section are all about this swimming pool.

Look at the picture. Can you think up any word problems about this swimming pool?

Picture problems

1 Rohan is 120 cm tall. Is there any part of the pool where he will not be able to stand safely?

2 Is it more than 90 minutes until it is half price?

3 Which of these is a sensible estimate for the length of the pool: 20 cm, 1 km, 100 m, 20 m or 2 m?

4 My friend is not wearing a red hat and is not standing next to the person in the blue hat. What colour hat is my friend wearing?

Pattern problems

1 There are four swimmers, each wearing a different colour hat.

The swimming teacher lines up the swimmers in a different order every week, to make it fair.

a In what order are they in the picture?

b How many other orders can you find?

2 The swimmers have to learn five skills.

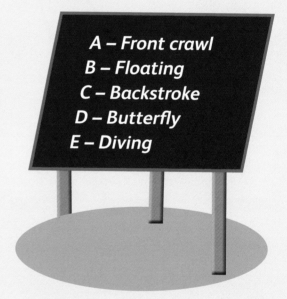

A – Front crawl
B – Floating
C – Backstroke
D – Butterfly
E – Diving

They only have time for three different activities each lesson. For example, in one lesson they learn front crawl, butterfly and diving.

How many lessons could there be with different mixes of activities?

Picture problems

Time	Activity
10.00–12.00	Fun swimming
12.00–1.00	Swimming lessons
1.00–3.00	Lane swimming
3.00–4.30	Races
4.30–6.00	Fun swimming

Prices

Adult $7

Child $4

Lessons $6

Half price after 4.30 p.m.

Try this

Make up three of your own word problems using the timetable and the price board.

1 Draw a picture to help solve each problem.

  a How much does it cost a family of two adults and three children to go swimming before 4.30 p.m?

  b If you had $20, how many lessons could you buy? How much change would you get?

  c If you went swimming with three friends at 5.00 p.m., would $10 be enough? How do you know?

  d How many minutes of fun swimming could you do in a day?

Calculating problems

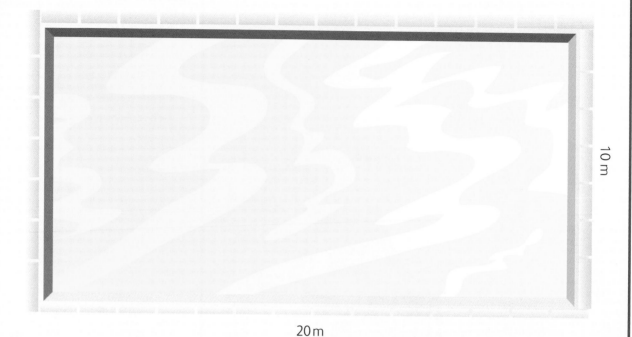

10 m

20 m

1 How many lengths would it take to swim 100 m? How many widths?

2 Theo swam 250 m. His brother swam 23 widths. Who swam the furthest?

3 Nina swam five widths and four lengths. Her sister swam four widths and five lengths. Who swam the furthest? By how much?

4 Dalia wants to swim 100 m. She has already swam 35 m. How much further does she need to swim?

5 Which is further to swim: two lengths or four widths?

Self-check

A Problem solving

1 This is how many vegetables Jo plants in 3 days.

Day 1: ten carrot plants

Day 2: eight potato plants

Day 3: five pumpkin plants

Jo carries on planting vegetables in this pattern each day.
How many vegetables will she have planted by Day 6?

2 Look at the picture of the swimming pool below. Answer the questions.

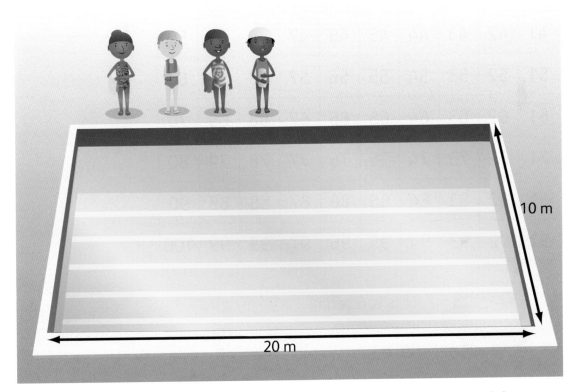

a If each learner in the picture swims eight laps of the pool, how many laps will this group swim altogether? Draw a picture and write a calculation to show how you worked out the answer.

b If the number of learners swimming eight laps is doubled, then how many laps would the learners swim altogether? Explain the method you used to work this out.

6a Number and place value

Explore

1	2	3	4	5	6	7	8	9	10
11	12	13	14	15	16	17	18	19	20
21	22	23	24	25	26	27	28	29	30
31	32	33	34	35	36	37	38	39	40
41	42	43	44	45	46	47	48	49	50
51	52	53	54	55	56	57	58	59	60
61	62	63	64	65	66	67	68	69	70
71	72	73	74	75	76	77	78	79	80
81	82	83	84	85	86	87	88	89	90
91	92	93	94	95	96	97	98	99	100

Key words
pattern
more
less
count on
count back
increase
decrease

This is a really interesting pattern.

I think I can see how the pattern continues.

Which numbers will be shaded yellow if the pattern continues?

(43) (52) (53) (60) (70) (99) (100)

Irina counts in fives and colours the numbers blue. What numbers does she colour?

Counting on and back

Learn

Work out the missing numbers in these patterns.

22	32	42	52		

		53	63	73	

		353	453	553	

Try this

Draw this number line.

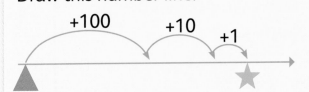

What number is ⭐ if 🔺 is 789?

What number is 🔺 if ⭐ is 789?

Practise

1 Write down the correct number for each letter. For example, **A is 51** and **B is 81**. That number track counts on in tens.

31	41	A	61	71	B

31	131	C	331	431	D

452	442	432	422	E	F

G	H	452	352	252	152

2 Answer these.

a 333 + 1 = ☐
   333 + 10 = ☐
   333 + 100 = ☐

b ☐ + 1 = 333
   ☐ + 10 = 333
   ☐ + 100 = 333

c 444 = 1 + ☐
   555 = 10 + ☐
   666 = 100 + ☐

d 333 − 1 = ☐
   333 − 10 = ☐
   333 − 100 = ☐

e ☐ − 1 = 333
   ☐ − 10 = 333
   ☐ − 100 = 33

f 777 = ☐ − 100
   888 = ☐ − 10
   999 = ☐ − 1

Multiplying by 10

Learn

What are the outputs from these different inputs?

INPUTS
3
8
13
28

Try this

How many solutions can you find to this? ☐ × 10 = ☐ + 10

Remember, the equals sign means 'is equal to'. Work out the calculation on one side of the equals sign, then the calculation on the other side. Both answers should match.

Practise

1 What are the outputs from these inputs?

5 15 25 55 75 95

2 What inputs are needed for these outputs?

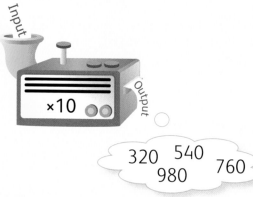

320 540 980 760

3 Two machines have been joined together. First, 5 is added, then the result is multiplied by 10. Match the inputs and outputs in the cloud below. One has been done for you.

If 25 is an input, 25 + 5 = 30 and 30 × 10 = 300. An input of 25 matches an output of 300.

25 300 20 350 250 30 31 360 42 470 410 36

Describing and continuing number patterns

Learn

1	2	3	4	5
6	7	8	9	10
11	12	13	14	15
16	17	18	19	20
21	22	23	24	25
26	27	28	29	30
31	32	33	34	35
36	37	38	39	40
41	42	43	44	45
46	47	48	49	50

What counting pattern is being shaded?
How do you know?

Practise

Use the 1–50 grid to answer these questions.

1 Will 50 be shaded or unshaded? Make a prediction. Then use counters to continue the pattern. Were you right? List all the numbers you covered up.

2 Start on 4, and count on in steps of 4. Will 50 be covered this time? Predict first, then check using counters. List all the numbers you covered up.

3 If you start on 2 and count on in 5s, which numbers in the bottom row will be covered?

Try this

Work out if the number 1 will be in your count if you count back in twos, threes, fours or fives from 50.

6b Comparing, ordering and rounding

Explore

What estimates can you make about this grid?

How many symbols are there?

Which is the most common?

Which is the least common?

Key words ⟳
greater than
less than
compare
order
rounding
nearest
estimate

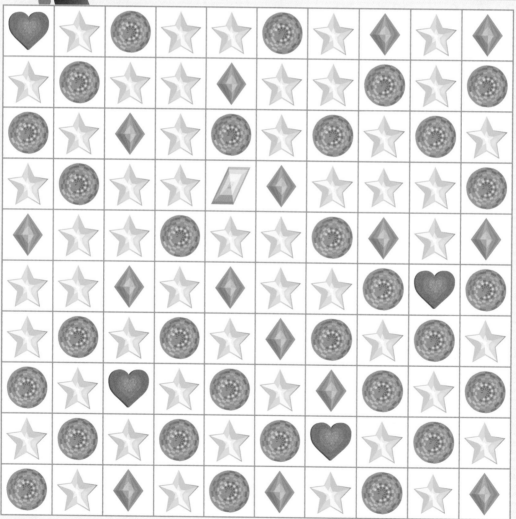

Greater than and less than

Learn

1 Where do the elephant and the goat fit in this pattern?

2 List four numbers for each box that would make these true.

▢ < 5 ▢ > 10

Practise

1 Write these numbers in order from smallest to largest.

a 19, 11, 17, 13, 15

b 19, 21, 17, 23, 15

c 91, 12, 71, 32, 51

d 51, 42, 33, 24, 15

2 Copy and complete by using the symbols < and >. The first two have been done for you.

a 12 < 20   b 21 > 12   c 21 ▢ 20   d 12 ▢ 10

e 20 ▢ 22   f 50 ▢ 60   g 50 ▢ 40   h 50 ▢ 51

i 50 ▢ 99   j 50 ▢ 49

3

Pick a number from the cloud to make these statements correct.
Use each number once only. Write the correct statements in your book.

a ☐ < 32   b 32 < ☐   c ☐ > 23

d 23 > ☐   e ☐ < 39   f ☐ > 35

▲ stands for my mystery number.
Here are some clues about my number:

▲ is an odd number.

▲ has 2 digits.

▲ > 90.

Write down the numbers that ▲ might be.

Rounding to the nearest 10

Learn

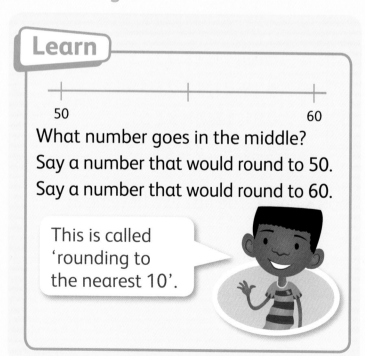

50   60

What number goes in the middle?
Say a number that would round to 50.
Say a number that would round to 60.

This is called 'rounding to the nearest 10'.

Try this

Use the digit cards to complete this inequality statement.

| 1 | 4 | 7 | 9 |

| | | > | | |

You can only use each card once in a solution.

How many different solutions can you make? Write them all in your book.

Practise

1 Copy the number line. Fill in three numbers that round to 40, and three numbers that round to 50.

Use this example to help you.

2 Round to the nearest 10.

a 23   b 32   c 46

d 64   e 69   f 96

I am thinking of an odd number. If I round it to the nearest 10, it is 30.

What other numbers could it be? Write down five possibilities.

I am thinking of an even number. If I round it to the nearest 10, it is 80. What other numbers could it be? Write down four solutions.

Try this

Charles is thinking of a number.

He doubles it.

Then he rounds it to the nearest 10, and gets 50.

Write all five possible solutions to this.

Think like a mathematician

If a number is exactly between two tens, like 45, then you round it up to the next ten. So 45 rounds to 50, and 75 rounds to 80.

Rounding to estimate the sum or difference

Learn

Look at this calculation.
38 + 53 = 501
I know it is wrong without even working out the answer exactly.

That is correct! You can use rounding to estimate the answer first.

38 + 53
rounds to ⟋   ⟍ rounds to
40   50
40 + 50 = 90

So the answer should be close to 90. Use a calculator to check.

Practise

1 Match each calculation to a sensible estimate.

Calculations	Estimates
42 + 49	40 + 50 = 90
32 + 39	30 + 40 = 70
51 + 51	50 + 50 = 100
12 + 67	10 + 70 = 80
45 + 55	50 + 60 = 110

2 One of each pair is wrong. Use estimates to find the mistakes.

a 81 − 27 = 24
   81 − 57 = 24

b 61 − 29 = 32
   71 − 29 = 32

c 92 − 31 = 51
   92 − 31 = 61

d 92 − 38 = 54
   92 − 58 = 54

e 98 − 69 = 29
   98 − 69 = 49

3 Use rounding to estimate how much money Irina spent last week. She had $1.50.
   ● On Monday she bought an apple for 9 cents.
   ● On Tuesday she bought an orange for 19 cents.
   ● On Wednesday she bought a banana for 39 cents.
   ● On Thursday she bought a pineapple for 49 cents.
   She found another $1 on Friday.
   Estimate how many oranges she can buy with the money she has now.

6c **Mental strategies**

Key words
strategy
multiple
multiply
divide
double
half

Explore

What are the different strategies for working out how many people, horses and cats there are?

Adding multiples of 5, 10 and 100

Learn

40 + 60 = 100

What has stayed the same, and what has changed in this second calculation?

Try this

Use your diagram pairs to help you answer these.

34 + ☐ = 100

35 + ☐ = 101

☐ + 65 = 101

Practise

1 Answer these.

a

1+ ☐ = 10

10 + ☐ = 100

100 + ☐ = 1000

b

☐ + 3 = 10

☐ + 30 = 100

☐ + 300 = 1000

c

10 = 6 + ☐

100 = 60 + ☐

1000 = 600 + ☐

d

10 − ☐ = 8

100 − ☐ = 80

1000 − ☐ = 800

e

10 − 5 = ☐

100 − 50 = ☐

1000 − 500 = ☐

2 Write calculations for these diagram pairs. The first has been done for you.

a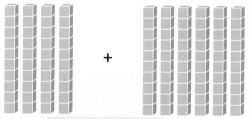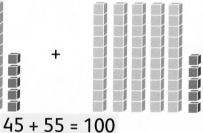

40 + 60 = 100   45 + 55 = 100

b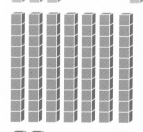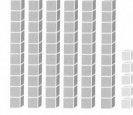

c

d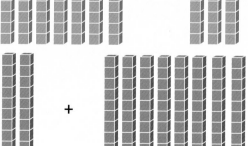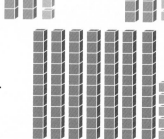

Division facts

Learn

What is the same and what is different about these diagrams?

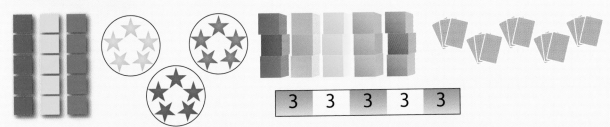

All these pictures show the fact that: 3 × 5 = 15 or 5 × 3 = 15.

If 15 is shared into three equal groups, how many in each group?

How many threes are there in 15?

What is 15 ÷ 3?

Can you work out any other division facts from the diagrams?

> You can say 15 divided by 3 is 5, because 5 × 3 = 15.

> 15 split into 3 is 5, because 5 lots of 3 is 15.

Practise

1 Use counters or cubes to work out these.

  a 12 split into four groups
      12 split into three groups

  b 20 split into ten groups
      20 split into two groups

     12 split into six groups
     12 split into two groups

     20 split into five groups
     20 split into four groups

  c Nine split into three groups
      Ten split into five groups. (This time predict the answer first.)

2 Complete these.

  a 15 ÷ 3 is 5, because 5 × 3 = 15   18 ÷ 3 is 6, because ____ × ____ = 18

  b 9 ÷ 3 is 3, because ____ × ____ = 9   24 ÷ 3 is ____, because 8 × 3 = 24

3 Draw arrays to show these multiplication facts.
  Write a division fact to go with each array.

   a 3 × 3 = 9

   b 4 × 4 = 16

   c 5 × 5 = 25

  What do you notice about each array?

4 Draw arrays for these.

   a 2 × 3 = 6

   b 5 × 2 = 10

   c 7 × 3 = 21

  Write two different division
  facts that go with each array.

  What is different about the
  arrays in question 3 and the
  arrays in question 4?

Try this

15 ÷ 5 = 3 because 5 × 3 = 15
Complete.
27 ÷ _____ is 3, because …
30 ÷ _____ is 5, because …
_____ ÷ 5 is 9, because …
_____ ÷ 5 is _____, because 5 × 7 = _____

Doubling and the 4× table

Learn

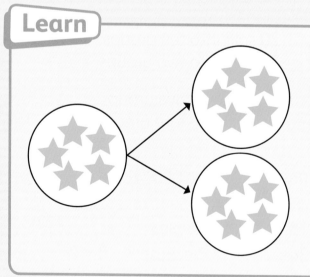

This diagram shows that double 5
is the same as 2 × 5.

Learn

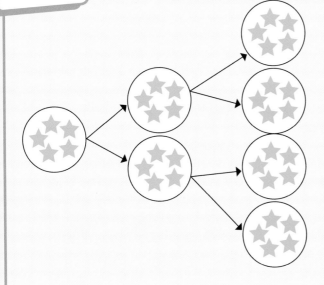

The diagram starts with one group of five.

This five is doubled to get two groups of five.

These groups of five are doubled to get four groups of five.

5 ⟶ 10 ⟶ 20

If you want to multiply a number by 4, you can just double and then double again.

Practise

1 Draw a double, double diagram for these.

  a 3 × 4

  b 7 × 4

2 Use your knowledge of doubles to answer these.

  a 6 × 4

  6 ⟶ [ ] ⟶ [ ] so 6 × 4 = [ ]

  b 8 × 4

  8 ⟶ [ ] ⟶ [ ] so 8 × 4 = [ ]

  c 11 × 4

  11 ⟶ [ ] ⟶ [ ] so 11 × 4 = [ ]

Try this

You can use the 'double, double' strategy to multiply any number by 4.

Use it to work out:

25 × 4

35 × 4

45 × 4

See how far you can carry on using this pattern.

Self-check

A Number and place value

1 Say if you count on or back for these number tracks. Say what the rule is each time.

29	32	35	38	41	44	47	50
925	825	725	625	525	425	325	225

2 Multiply each number in the list by 10. Say what changes for the number each time.

6	21	16	37	58	94	40	100

3 What is the same about the numbers in this list? How do these numbers change each time?

4	14	24	34	44	54	64	74	84	94

B Comparing, ordering and rounding

1 Write down a number that is < 58 and > 45.

2 Order these numbers from smallest to largest.

76	68	71	15	80	82

3 Choose three numbers from the list that round to 60 and three numbers that round to 80.

69	79	62	71	67	75	65	64	61	66	77

4 Which estimate in the list matches the calculation 32 + 39?

30 + 40 = 70	30 + 30 = 60	30 + 20 = 50	30 + 10 = 40

C Mental strategies

1 Match these division facts with the multiplication facts.

$60 \div 6 = 10$	$18 \div 2 = 9$	$35 \div 5 = 7$

a $9 \times 2 = 18$ b $7 \times 5 = 35$ c $10 \times 6 = 60$

2 Draw a diagram to show how to do this double calculation.
   $5 \longrightarrow 10 \longrightarrow 20$ so $5 \times 4 = 20$

3 Work out these calculations.
   a 45 + 45   b 25 × 4   c 50 + 50

⟳ 7a Money

Explore

Key words ⟳
change
dollar
cent
amount
cost
estimate
strategy

I bought these presents for my family. I spent $10. Each present cost a different amount.

I bought these presents for my family. I also spent $10.

How much did each present cost?
Work out four different solutions.

Number stories

Juice Cafe menu

	Small	Medium	Large
Apple juice	25c	40c	55c
Peach juice	35c	50c	65c
Orange juice	45c	60c	75c
Mango juice	55c	70c	85c

If you want a smoothie, add 50c to the price.

Learn

Irina has $1 to buy a juice for herself and Felix. Felix wants a medium peach juice.

Which drink(s) can Irina pay for with the money she has left?

$$\$\,1\,\$ - 50¢ = \boxed{}$$

Try this

I bought three drinks and Felix bought two drinks. We both spent the same. What drinks could we have bought?

Practise

1 Look at the menu. Work out the cost of each order. The first one has been done for you.

  a A small apple juice and a medium orange juice

     25 c + 60 c = 85 c

  b Two small peach juices

  c A medium apple juice and a small mango juice

  d Three medium peach juices.

2 Felix bought two drinks and the cost was exactly $1.

  What five different drink combinations could he have bought?

3 Which costs more?

  a A medium apple smoothie or a large mango juice

  b A medium peach smoothie or two small orange juices

  c A medium and a large apple juice or a large apple smoothie

  d Three medium peach juices or two medium peach smoothies

  e Three medium peach juices or a small apple juice, a small orange juice and a small peach juice.

Estimates and change

Learn

The Juice Cafe has added another type of juice to its menu.

Guava juice	Small	Medium	Large
	49c	99c	$1.99

What is the cost of three medium guava juice drinks?

You get 1c change from $1 for one drink.

You get 2c change from $2 when you buy two medium drinks.

How much change would you get if you bought three medium drinks with

 ?

Practise

1 Work out the change you will get each time.

	I bought	I used these coins and notes
a	Three small guava juices	50c 50c 50c
b	One small and one medium guava juice	50c $ 1 $
c	Two large guava juices	$ 1 $ $ 1 $ $ 1 $ $ 1 $
d	One small, one medium and one large guava juice	$ 1 $ $ 1 $ $ 1 $ $ 1 $

Try this

Estimate how many guava drinks of each size you could buy with $10. Round each price to the nearest $1 or 50c, then use this to help you estimate.

7b **Mass**

Explore

Key words

gram
kilogram
scale
interval
mass
units
weigh
weight

How much is each animal carrying?

How can you make sensible estimates?

Grams and kilograms

Learn

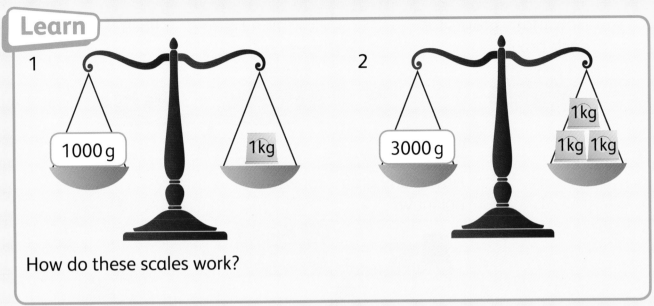

1   1000 g   1kg

2   3000 g   1kg   1kg   1kg

How do these scales work?

Practise

1 Work out what is needed to balance each scale.

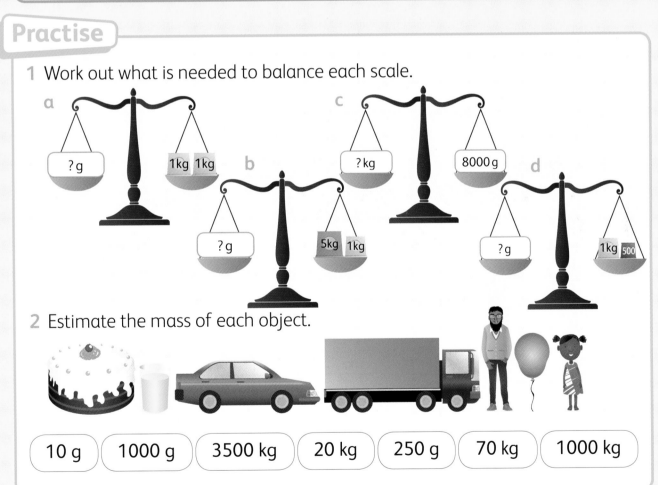

a   ? g   1kg 1kg

b   ? g   5kg 1kg

c   ? kg   8000 g

d   ? g   1kg 500

2 Estimate the mass of each object.

| 10 g | 1000 g | 3500 kg | 20 kg | 250 g | 70 kg | 1000 kg |

Try this

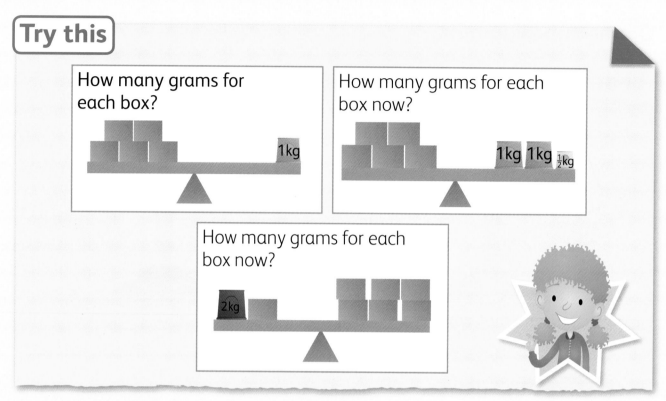

How many grams for each box?

1kg

How many grams for each box now?

1kg 1kg ½kg

How many grams for each box now?

2kg

Reading scales and solving problems

Learn

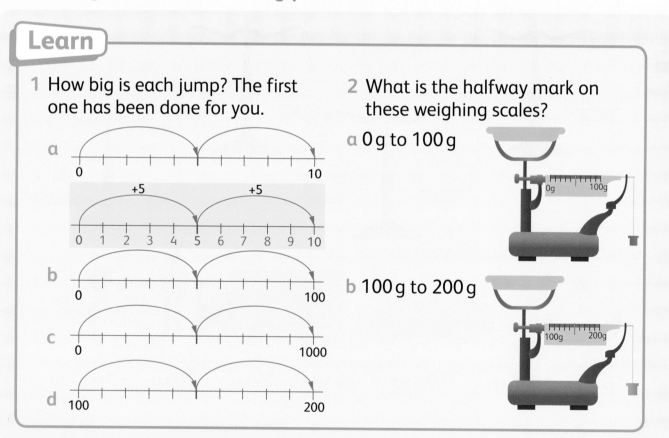

1 How big is each jump? The first one has been done for you.

a

0   10

+5   +5

0 1 2 3 4 5 6 7 8 9 10

b

0   100

c

0   1000

d 100   200

2 What is the halfway mark on these weighing scales?

a 0 g to 100 g

0g   100g

b 100 g to 200 g

100g   200g

Practise

1 How big is each jump?

a   0   20

b   10   20

c   200   300

d   20   30

e   2000   3000

2 What mass does each blue line show?

A   0 kg 100g 200g 300g 400g 500g 600g 700g 800g 900g 1 kg

B   0 kg 1 kg 2 kg 3 kg 4 kg 5 kg 6 kg

C   0 kg 1 kg 2 kg 3 kg 4 kg 5 kg 6 kg

D   0 kg 100g 200g 300g 400g 500g 600g 700g 800g 900g 1 kg

E   0 kg 100g 200g 300g 400g 500g 600g 700g 800g 900g 1 kg

F   0 kg 100g 200g 300g 400g 500g 600g 700g 800g 900g 1 kg

3 a Which bird is the heaviest?
  b Which bird has a mass closest to 200 g?
  c How much more mass does the heaviest bird have than the lightest bird?
  d Which two birds would have a mass of 500 g together?
  e Which three birds would have a mass of 525 g altogether?

7c Time

Key words

time
second
minute
hour
day
week
month
year
calendar

Explore

These are some of the objects people used to tell the time before we had clocks.
How do you think they work?

How are modern clocks better at telling the time?
What facts do you know about seconds, minutes and hours?

Reading a calendar

Learn

JANUARY						
M	T	W	T	F	S	S
	1	2	3	4	5	6
7	8	9	10	11	12	13
14	15	16	17	18	19	20
21	22	23	24	25	26	27
28	29	30	31			

Today is 9 January. The red cross shows the date of my birthday.
How many days until my birthday?
How many weeks?

Practise

JANUARY						
M	T	W	T	F	S	S
	1	2	3	4	5	6
7	8	9	10	11	12	13
14	15	16	17	18	19	20
21	22	23	24	25	26	27̶
28	29	30	31			

FEBRUARY						
M	T	W	T	F	S	S
				1	2	3
4	5̶	6	7	8	9	10
11	12	13	14	15	16	1̶7̶
18	19	20	21	22	23	24
25	26	2̶7̶	28			

Key			
×	Felix's birthday	×	School play
×	Irina's birthday	×	Football match

1 What day of the week is it:

   a Felix's birthday?

   b Irina's birthday?

   c the day before the school play?

   d the day after the football match?

   e a week after Irina's birthday?

   f a week after Felix's birthday?

2 Today is 30 January. How long is it:

   a until the school play?

   b until Irina's birthday?

   c until the football match?

   d until 1 March?

   e since Felix's birthday?

   f since 15 January?

   g since a week before Felix's birthday?

3 How long is it:

   a between the two birthdays?

   b between the school play and the football match?

   c from the start of January until the end of February?

   d from a week before Felix's birthday, until a week after Irina's birthday?

   e from a week after Felix's birthday, until a week before Irina's birthday?

   f from the football match until the next match, which is on 20 March?

Try this

We started practising for the school play on 12 December. For how many days did we practise? We did not practise on weekends!

The difference between two times

Learn

How long did it take Hans to get to school?

This number line is a useful way to work out the journey time.

7.55　8.00　　　　　　　　　　8.20

How many minutes is each jump? What is the total time?

7.55　8.00　　　　　　　　　　8.20

Practise

School timetable	
8.45 a.m.	School starts – registration
9.30 a.m.	Mathematics
10.30 a.m.	Break
10.45 a.m.	Science
11.30 a.m.	English
12.15 p.m.	Lunch
1.05 p.m.	History
2.00 p.m.	Physical education
2.50 p.m.	Assembly
3.10 p.m.	School finishes

1 How many minutes from start to finish?

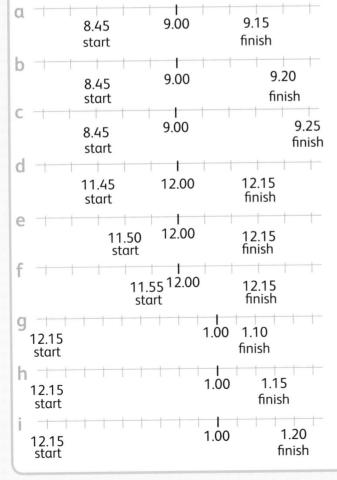

2 These clocks show the time in class. Use the timetable to work out how long it is until the next lesson begins.

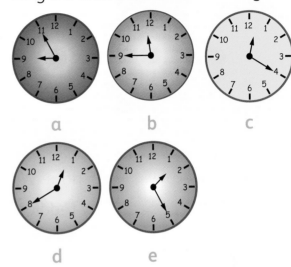

3 How long until the next lesson begins?

87

Self-check

A Money

90c

$1.50

1 Felix and Irina buy two teddies and one paint set at the toy shop. They pay with a $5 note. Work out how much change they get.

2 Estimate how many teddies Felix and Irina can buy for $10. Now work it out. How close was your estimate?

3 Write your own word problem to go with this calculation.

$1.99 + 25c + 60c = ☐

B Measuring mass

1 Match the grams in Row 1 with the kilograms in Row 2.

Row 1	500 g	3 000 g	1 000 g	8 000 g	5 000 g

Row 2	5 kg	3 kg	$\frac{1}{2}$ kg	1 kg	8 kg

2 Write down the halfway mark between these measurements.
   a 100 g to 200 g
   b 10 kg to 20 kg

3 If one mouse has a mass of 200 g, what is the total mass of five mice? Show the method you used to work this out. Write the answer in grams and in kilograms.

C Time

1 If today is 4 January, how many days until 25 January?
How many weeks?

JANUARY						
M	T	W	T	F	S	S
	1	2	3	4	5	6
7	8	9	10	11	12	13
14	15	16	17	18	19	20
21	22	23	24	25	26	27
28	29	30	31			

2 Look at the clocks. How many minutes or hours have passed?

a

b

3 The zoo opens at 8.00 in the morning and closes at 4.30 in the afternoon. For how many hours and minutes does the zoo stay open each day?

Unit 8   Number and problem solving

8a Addition and subtraction

Explore

Look at the first pyramid.
Can you see how the numbers are connected?

Use the rules you discover to work out the missing numbers in the second and third pyramids.

Can you think of two different ways to work out what number should be in the yellow circle?

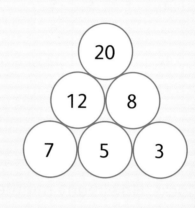

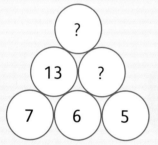

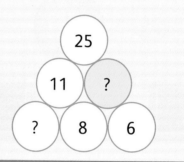

Key words
add
addition
sum
total
subtract
take away
minus
inverse
jottings
strategy

Jottings and mental methods

Learn

Felix uses a mental strategy to find the number that is missing from the yellow circle.

The calculation is 21 + 32.

Felix turns the calculation into: 32 + 21.

Then he adds 20 to 32 to get 52.

Then he adds 1 to 52: 52 + 1.

He gets the answer 53. Work out the two remaining missing numbers.

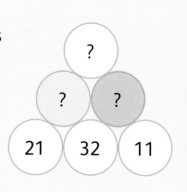

Irina uses a number line to find the number
missing from the blue circle in the second pyramid.

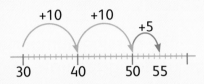

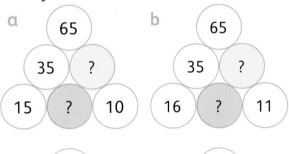

Irina works out what to add to 30 to reach 55.

The blue circle must be 25, because 30 + 25 = 55.

Write down two different ways to work out the number missing from the
yellow circle.

Practise

1 What number is missing from the
yellow circle?

a
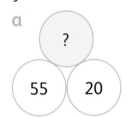
| ? |
| 55 | 20 |

b
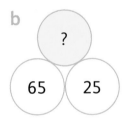
| ? |
| 65 | 25 |

c
| ? |
| 65 | 24 |

d
| 90 |
| 60 | ? |

e
| 90 |
| 70 | ? |

f
| 90 |
| 89 | ? |

2 Work out the numbers missing from
the yellow and blue circles.

a
| 65 |
| 35 | ? |
| 15 | ? | 10 |

b
| 65 |
| 35 | ? |
| 16 | ? | 11 |

c
| 120 |
| ? | 80 |
| 10 | 30 | ? |

d
| 88 |
| ? | 55 |
| ? | 22 | 33 |

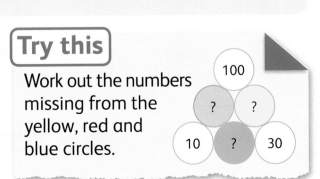

Try this

Work out the numbers
missing from the
yellow, red and
blue circles.

| 100 |
| ? | ? |
| 10 | ? | 30 |

Adding and subtracting two- and three-digit numbers

Learn

Write down the calculation that this number line shows.

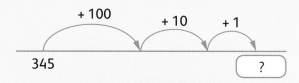

+ 100   + 10   + 1

345   ?

The missing number can be found by doing separate calculations and writing these down as you go.

$345 + 100 = 445$
$445 + 10 = 455$
$455 + 1 = 456$

Practise

1 Answer these.

a $30 + 20 =$ ☐
   $135 + 20 =$ ☐
   $30 - 20 =$ ☐
   $135 - 20 =$ ☐

b $50 + 30 =$ ☐
   $155 + 30 =$ ☐
   $50 - 30 =$ ☐
   $155 - 30 =$ ☐

c $50 + 100 =$ ☐
   $135 + 200 =$ ☐
   $150 - 100 =$ ☐
   $530 - 300 =$ ☐

2 What is the missing number in each number line?

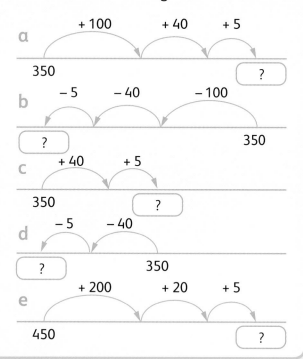

a   + 100   + 40   + 5
    350   ?

b   − 5   − 40   − 100
    ?   350

c   + 40   + 5
    350   ?

d   − 5   − 40
    ?   350

e   + 200   + 20   + 5
    450   ?

Try this

What is the pattern connecting all these calculations?

Use it to work out the answers. Jottings or number lines can help you.

a $1 + 2 + 3 + 4$
b $10 + 20 + 30 + 40$
c $11 + 21 + 31 + 41$
d $9 + 19 + 29 + 39$
e $100 + 200 + 300 + 400$
f $99 + 199 + 299 + 399$

Using the inverse

Learn

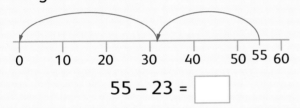

$\square$ + ▮▮ = ▮▮▮▮

$\square$ + 23 = 55

0 10 20 30 40 50 55 60

You can work out the missing number by using the inverse.

0 10 20 30 40 50 55 60

$55 - 23 = \square$

Try this

Pascal thinks of a number, adds 100 and then takes away 1. His answer is 123.

Nataliya thinks of a number, adds 100, takes away 10, and then adds 1. Her answer is 123.

What are Pascal and Nataliya's starting numbers?

Practise

1 Solve these by using the inverse.

a 0 10 20 30 40 50 60 70
$\square$ + 33 = 67

b 0 10 20 30 40 50 60 70
$\square$ − 33 = 24

c 0 10 20 30 40 50 60 70
$\square$ + 43 = 66

d 0 10 20 30 40 50 60 70
$\square$ − 43 = 25

e 0 10 20 30 40 50 60 70
$\square$ + 53 = 65

f 0 10 20 30 40 50 60 70
$\square$ − 53 = 26

2 Draw number lines to find the missing numbers.

a $\square$ + 123 = 357
b $\square$ − 123 = 357
c $\square$ + 133 = 345
d $\square$ − 133 = 345
e $\square$ + 123 = 246
f $\square$ − 245 = 123

8b Multiplication and division

Explore

These 100 number squares have been torn off at 30.
Look at the patterns and the numbers.

a

1	2	3	4	5	6	7	8	9	10
11	12	13	14	15	16	17	18	19	20
21	22	23	24	25	26	27	28	29	30

b

1	2	3	4	5	6	7	8	9	10
11	12	13	14	15	16	17	18	19	20
21	22	23	24	25	26	27	28	29	30

c

1	2	3	4	5	6	7	8	9	10
11	12	13	14	15	16	17	18	19	20
21	22	23	24	25	26	27	28	29	30

d

1	2	3	4	5	6	7	8	9	10
11	12	13	14	15	16	17	18	19	20
21	22	23	24	25	26	27	28	29	30

e

1	2	3	4	5	6	7	8	9	10
11	12	13	14	15	16	17	18	19	20
21	22	23	24	25	26	27	28	29	30

f

1	2	3	4	5	6	7	8	9	10
11	12	13	14	15	16	17	18	19	20
21	22	23	24	25	26	27	28	29	30

Work out what numbers would be highlighted in the next row of each
number square. Can you work these out by looking at the patterns?

Multiplication facts

Learn

What multiplication does this
picture show?

How could you find out how
many dots in total?

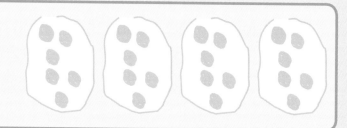

Practise

1 Draw pictures for these multiplications. The first one has been done for you.

a 3 × 5 = 15 ●●● ●●● ●●● ●●● ●●●   b 5 × 3 = ☐   c 7 × 3 = ☐

d 4 × 5 = ☐   e 5 × 4 = ☐   f 7 × 4 = ☐

g 6 × 5 = ☐   h 5 × 6 = ☐   i 8 × 4 = ☐

2 Answer true or false. If false, show why. The first one has been done for you.

a 3 × 4 = 14

false
●●● ●●● ●●● ●●●
3 × 4 = 12

b 4 × 3 = 12   c 5 × 6 = 30   d 6 × 5 = 25

e 7 × 4 = 17   f 4 × 7 = 28   g 2 × 9 = 18

h 9 × 2 = 18   i 5 × 5 = 20   j 3 × 3 = 6

3 Some of these function machines are broken. What should their outputs be?

a 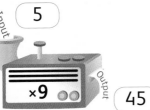 Input 5 ×9 Output 45

b  Input 2 ×9 Output 18

c  Input 7 ×9 Output 70

d  Input 3 ×9 Output 27

e  Input 4 ×9 Output 36

f  Input 1 ×9 Output 9

g  Input 10 ×9 Output 90

h  Input 6 ×9 Output 50

Try this

Write down the two-digit multiples of 9 in a list. Look for patterns in the digits. What happens when you add the digits in each number?

Multiplication and division

Learn

I know that
4 × 5 = 20.

You can use that fact to solve these number problems.

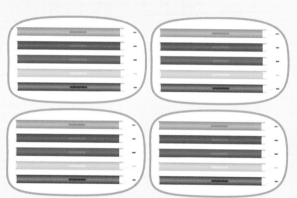

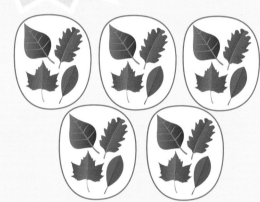

Share 20 colouring pens between 4 tables. How many on each table?
20 ÷ 4 = 5

20 leaves are put into groups of 4. How many groups?
20 ÷ 4 = 5

Practise

1 Draw an array for each of these.

  a 3 × 2   b 3 × 3   c 4 × 2

  d 4 × 3   e 5 × 2   f 5 × 3

  Write two division facts to go with each array.

  One array has only one division fact. Which is it?

2 There are 6 tables in a classroom. Share these out equally among the tables.

  a 30 pencils   b 24 rulers

  c 18 stools   d 36 pens

  e 12 paintbrushes   f 60 stickers

Divisions with remainders

Learn

Jenny has 17 cubes. She puts them into groups of 5.

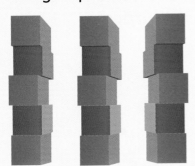

She has 3 groups of 5, with 2 cubes left over.

17 ÷ 5 = 3, remainder 2

Try this

Make a list of all the numbers less than 100 that leave a remainder of 1 when you divide by 10.

What do you notice?

Now make a list of all the numbers less than 60 that leave a remainder of 1 when you divide by 5.

What do you notice?

Practise

1 Use cubes or counters to solve these.

a 16 ÷ 4   b 24 ÷ 4

c 18 ÷ 3   d 24 ÷ 3

e 18 ÷ 6   f 24 ÷ 6

g 16 ÷ 2   h 24 ÷ 2

2 Find the remainder.

a 17 ÷ 4   b 25 ÷ 4

c 20 ÷ 3   d 26 ÷ 3

e 20 ÷ 6   f 26 ÷ 6

g 16 ÷ 3   h 23 ÷ 2

3 Complete each of these divisions so that they have a remainder. The first one has been done for you.

a 16 ÷ ☐   16 ÷ 3 = 5 remainder 1

b 21 ÷ ☐   c 25 ÷ ☐

d 35 ÷ ☐   e ☐ ÷ 2

f ☐ ÷ 3   g ☐ ÷ 4

h ☐ ÷ 5   i ☐ ÷ 6

j ☐ ÷ 9

8c Calculation problems

Explore

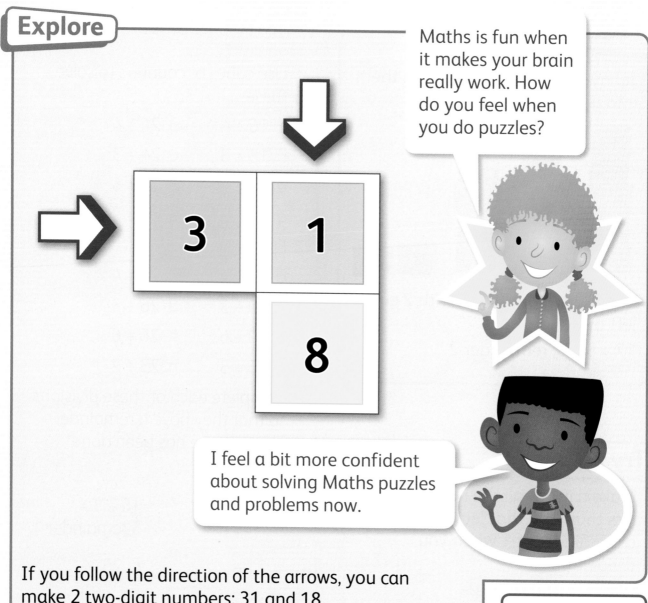

Maths is fun when it makes your brain really work. How do you feel when you do puzzles?

I feel a bit more confident about solving Maths puzzles and problems now.

If you follow the direction of the arrows, you can make 2 two-digit numbers: 31 and 18.

What is 31 add 18?

Move the three cards around. List the other totals you can make.

Which card could you change for another card to make the total exactly 50?

Which card could you change for another card to make the total exactly 60?

Key words

puzzle
problem
strategy
predict
pattern
rule

Testing number rules

Learn

Hundreds	Tens	Ones
5	5	5

What does each digit stand for in the grid above?

Which digit would change if you did these calculations?

555 – 1

555 + 100

I think that if you add 10 to a number, you only have to change the tens digit.

True
146 + 10

False
199 + 10

Write down two more calculations that would change only the tens digit.

Practise

If you take away 10 from a number, only the tens digit changes.

1 Find five different calculations for each circle.

True

False

If you add 1 to a number, you get a number that ends in a zero.

2 Write down five different calculations that show when this statement is true. Find five that show when it is false.

When you divide a number by 10, you get a remainder of 1.

3 Write down ten calculations that show when this statement is true.

Try this

When you halve a number, the answer is an odd number.

When you double a number, the answer is an even number.

Test these statements with different numbers. What do you see?

99

Patterns in word problems

What strategy would you use to solve this word problem?

Kiran has 20 sweets. He gives five of them to Tara.

Kiran has the most sweets.
20 sweets – 5 sweets = 15 sweets
or: 5 is less than half of 20, so Kiran must have more than half left.

1 Explain how to solve these word problems.

   a Kiran has 200 sweets. He gives five of them to Tara.

   b Kiran has 20 sweets. He gives 11 of them to Tara.

   c Kiran has 24 sweets. He gives 11 of them to Tara.

   d Kiran has 49 sweets. He gives 25 of them to Tara.

   e Kiran has 51 sweets. He gives 25 of them to Tara.

2 What strategies could you use to solve these?

   a I had to chop 100 cm from the top of my tree. Now it is 253 cm tall. How tall was it to start with?

   b I had to chop 50 cm from the top of my tree. Now it is 253 cm tall. How tall was it to start with?

   c I had to chop 100 cm from the top of my tree. It was 253 cm to start with. How tall is it now?

   d I had to chop 50 cm from the top of my tree. It was 253 cm to start with. How tall is it now?

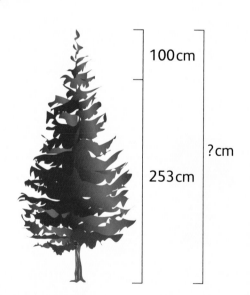

100cm

253cm

?cm

Predicting answers

Learn

Put a digit card in each box to find the total of the two numbers.

Move the digits to get a larger total.

Predict whether you can move the digits around to get a total greater than 100.

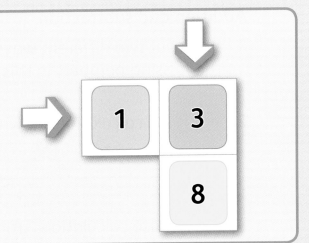

Practise

1 Use these sets of digit cards to make the largest total each time.

Predict whether the total will be more or less than 100.

a **2** **3** **4**

b **3** **4** **5**

c **6** **5** **4**

d **1** **1** **5**

e **5** **5** **1**

f **5** **0** **5**

2

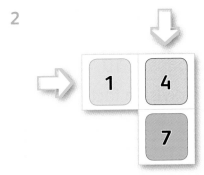

a Change one digit to get a total of exactly 50.

b Now change another digit to get a total of exactly 60.

c Now change another digit to get a total of 62.

Try this

Choose your own three digits. Aim for a total of exactly 100. How many different solutions can you find?

Self-check

A Addition and subtraction

1 Work out two different ways of finding the missing numbers in this pyramid.

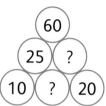

2 Write the calculation shown on this number line.

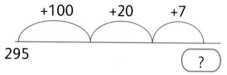

3 Solve these calculations using the inverse.

a [ ] + 24 = 82   b [ ] − 33 = 30

B Multiplication and division

1 Write the multiplication calculations. Work out the answers.
   a Three groups of 9   b Six groups of 5
   c Two groups of 10   d Four groups of 8

2 Write two division facts for this array.

3 Share 28 straws among six groups of learners. What is the remainder?

C Calculation problems

1 What happens to each of these numbers when you add 100? What stays the same each time?

412	175	290	318	561	803

2 Write two different strategies you could use to solve this word problem.

Max collected 16 stickers in May. In April, he collected double this number. How many stickers did Max collect in April?

3 Make the largest total you can with these digit cards. Predict if it will be more or less than 50.

2 3 5

Unit 9 Handling data and problem solving

9a Sorting numbers and shapes

Growing patterns

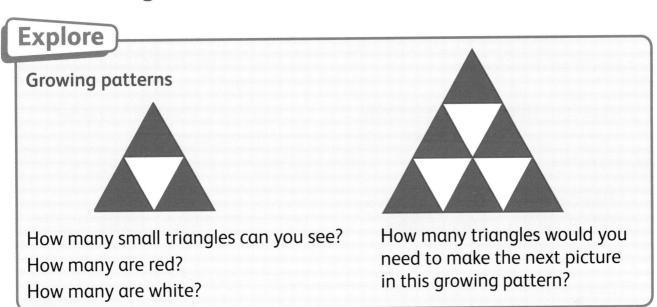

How many small triangles can you see?
How many are red?
How many are white?

How many triangles would you need to make the next picture in this growing pattern?

Properties and sorting

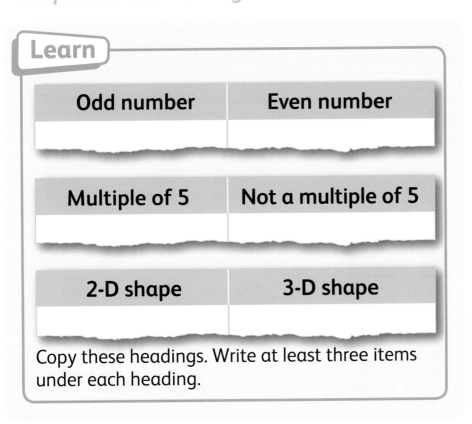

Odd number	Even number

Multiple of 5	Not a multiple of 5

2-D shape	3-D shape

Copy these headings. Write at least three items under each heading.

Key words

regular
irregular
triangle
square
quadrilateral
side
corner

Practise

1 Draw these tables. Now write the letter of each shape under the correct table heading. The first one has been done for you.

Has four sides	Does not have four sides
A, B, H, I	

Has curved sides	Does not have curved sides

Even number of corners	Odd number of corners

I know the name	I do not know the name

2 Draw a shape that has:

a four corners

b four corners and all four sides the same length

c four corners and all four sides different lengths

d four corners and opposite sides the same length

e four corners and no right angles.

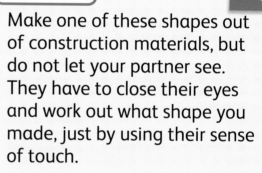

Try this

Make one of these shapes out of construction materials, but do not let your partner see. They have to close their eyes and work out what shape you made, just by using their sense of touch.

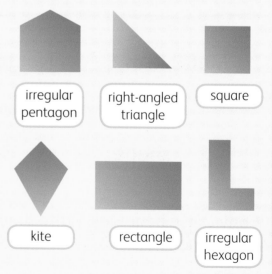

irregular pentagon

right-angled triangle

square

kite

rectangle

irregular hexagon

Carroll and Venn diagrams

Learn

Think of two or more animals to go in each section of this Carroll diagram.

Where would your favourite animal go?

Are there any living creatures that do not fit in this diagram?

	Has legs	Does not have legs
Lives on land		
Does not live on land		

Practise

1 Copy the Carroll diagram. Write the names of the shapes below that fit in each section.

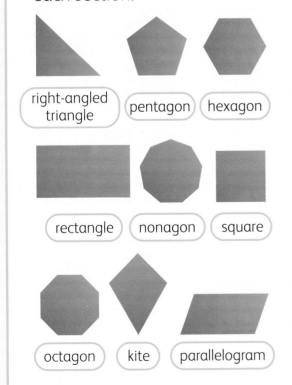

right-angled triangle   pentagon   hexagon

rectangle   nonagon   square

octagon   kite   parallelogram

	Odd number of sides	Even number of sides
Fewer than five corners		
Five corners or more		

105

2 Write the letter of each shape that is in the wrong place.

	Orange	Not orange
Quadrilateral	A ■ B ▲ C ⬠	D ▭ E ⬠ F ⬡
Not a quadrilateral	G ▲ H ⬡ I ⬠	J ▲ K ⬡ L ◆

3 Write the headings.

	Heading A	Heading B
Heading C	⬠	⬠
Heading D	⬠ ■	▲ ▰

Think like a mathematician

If you get stuck when sorting shapes, find or make the shape you need.
Even just drawing a sketch can help you to notice its properties.

Try this

Why will one of the sections of this diagram always be empty?

	Odd number of corners	Even number of corners
Quadrilateral		
Not a quadrilateral		

9b Charts, graphs and tables

Explore

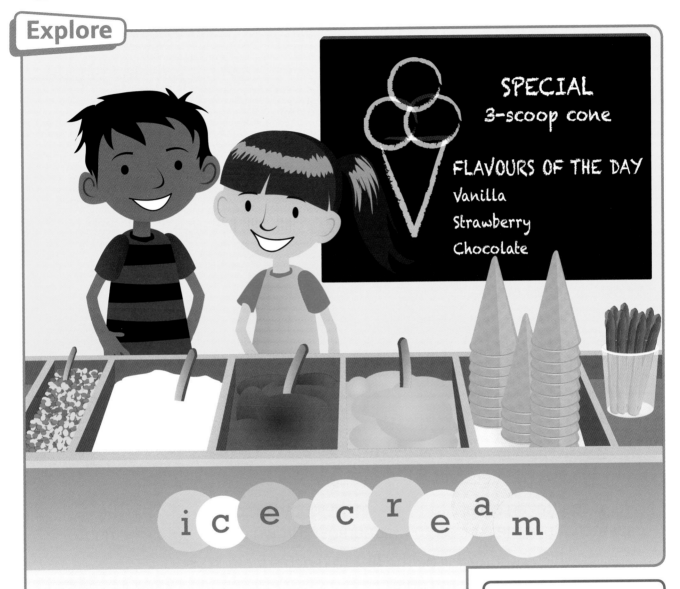

SPECIAL
3-scoop cone

FLAVOURS OF THE DAY
Vanilla
Strawberry
Chocolate

i c e c r e a m

Sunil and Maya are choosing ice cream flavours for their three-scoop cones. They can have chocolate, vanilla and strawberry.

How many different combinations can you make?

What would be a good way to record all your ideas?

Key words

data

tally chart

pictogram

bar chart

list

table

Collecting information

Learn

Three friends collected information about how many times a bird fed from their birdfeeder in one afternoon.

38 |||||||||||||||||||||||||||||||||||||

36 |||| |||| |||| |||| |||| |||| |||| |

They decided to use tally marks to keep count.

Did they all count accurately?

Which person used the best strategy for recording?

25 ||||| ||||| ||||| ||||| |||||

Practise

1 You need six counters and a 1–6 spinner.

Put a counter on each 'Start' box on the board on page 109. Spin the spinner. Move the counter for the number thrown one space to the right.

Predict which counter will be the first to reach square 10.
Then play to see if you are right.

I predict that counter 1 will be the first to reach square 10, because that is the first number on the spinner.

I think it will not be counter 6, because it is really hard to spin a 6.

Start	Total	1	2	3	4	5	6	7	8	9	10

Compare your result with the rest of your class. Is there one counter that wins more often than the others?

2 You need two 1–6 spinners.

Spin both spinners and add the scores together.

Work in pairs. One person spins the spinners and records the totals in a tally chart. The other person keeps a tally of how many times you have spun the spinners. After 50 spins, see which total is the most common.

Now swap. Play the game again. See if the same number wins.

Compare your results with the rest of the class.

Try this

Play one of these spinner races.

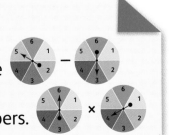

- Roll two 1–6 spinners and find the difference between the two numbers.
- Roll two 1–6 spinners and multiply the numbers.

Solving problems about charts

Learn

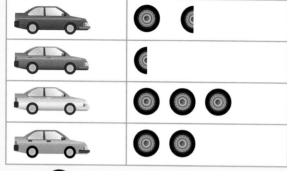

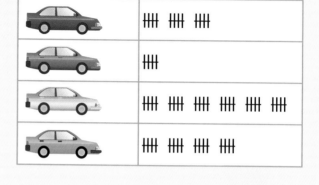

Key: ⊚ = 10 cars

Cars in a car park

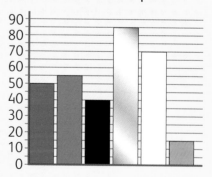

These charts record the number of cars in a car park. What is the same and what is different about the charts?

Practise

Use the charts above to answer these questions.

1 a Which is the most common colour?

  b Which is the least common colour?

  c How many cars are there in total?

  d How many more silver cars are there than blue cars?

  e How many more orange cars are there than red cars?

Try this

Turn this bar graph into a pictogram.
Use the key: ⊚ = 20 cars
Invent three word problems to go with it.

Cars in a car park

Self-check

A Sorting numbers and shapes

Sort these 2-D shapes in each section of the Carroll diagram.

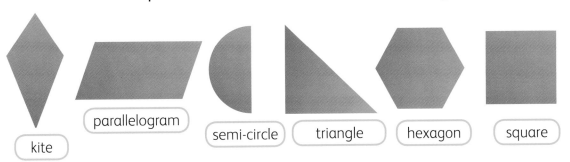

kite
parallelogram
semi-circle
triangle
hexagon
square

	Has four sides	Does not have four sides
Has a right angle		
Does not have a right angle		

B Charts, graphs and tables

1 Do a class survey on the transport each learner uses to get to school. Show the information you collected as a tally chart, in a table and as a bar graph.

2 Which forms of transport are the most popular, and the least popular in your class?

3 If double the number of learners use the most popular transport, how many learners will this be? Show how you worked this out.

10a Problem solving

Explore

The problems in this section are about this underwater scene.
Write down three word problems related to this picture.

Picture problems

1 How tall do you think the seaweed is? Make an estimate based on clues from the picture.

2 Estimate how deep the sea is in this picture. Does your estimate for the height of seaweed help?

3 Estimate how long the submarine is.

4 Write two different calculations you could use to work out the number of octopus tentacles in the picture.

5 Draw an array to show how many starfish tentacles there are in the picture.

Pattern problems

These show two sides of a red spotfish and a blue spotfish.

How many spots are there on a red spotfish?

1 Diver A caught 3 red spotfish and 2 blue spotfish.

Diver B caught 2 red spotfish and 3 blue spotfish.

Whose catch had the most spots altogether?

2 Diver C counted all the spots on his fish. There were 11 in total.

How many of each fish did he catch?

3 Diver D counted all the spots on her fish. There were 17 in total.

How many of each fish did she catch?

There are two solutions. Can you find both of them?

4 Diver E caught some red spotfish and blue spotfish. In total there were 30 spots.

How many of each fish did he catch?

Find two solutions to this problem.

5 Diver F's aim is to collect fish with 20 spots on Monday, 19 spots on Tuesday and 18 spots on Wednesday.

Can he do it?

Logic problems

1 Some explorers find treasure.

They find twice as many rubies as diamonds.

There are four times as many gold coins as sapphires.

There are five fewer emeralds than sapphires.

There are half as many rubies as gold coins.

There are 18 rubies.

Work out how many there are of each kind.

How many pieces of treasure are there altogether?

2 Copy and complete the square so that there are five different kinds of treasure in each row and column.

Use different colour cubes or counters to represent each type of treasure.

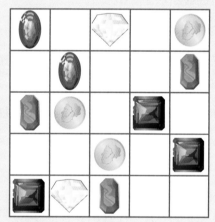

Key	
	Ruby
	Diamond
	Sapphire
	Emerald
	Gold coin

Try this

Make your own grid puzzle with the treasure in a different order.
Use different colour cubes or counters to help you invent the grid.

Hide between five and ten pieces of the treasures.
See if your partner can work out what is missing.
Draw the puzzle on a grid to share with the rest of the class.

Self-check

Problem solving

A toy shop has a promotion on sets of toy cars.

1 Write two different calculations you could use to work out the number of wheels in total for the toy cars in the picture.

2 If the toy shop sells ten sets of toy cars on Friday, and double the sets on Saturday, how many sets will they sell altogether?

3 The shopkeeper sells twice as many sets of toy cars on Sunday as she sells on Friday and Saturday together. How many sets of toy cars are sold in total on these three days?

11a Number and place value

Key words

digit
less than
more than
order
rounding
pattern

Explore

Are these statements always, sometimes or never true?
Choose two that are sometimes true. Show when they
are true and when they are not.

> When you double a
> number, the answer
> ends in a zero.

When you
add 5 to a
number, the
answer ends
in a zero.

If you multiply
a number by 10,
your answer has
three digits.

If you double
a two-digit
number,
you get a
four-digit
answer.

When you subtract 9 from a number,
the answer ends in a 5.

When you halve
a number,
the answer ends
in a 5.

Ordering numbers

How many different ways can you arrange the digit cards to make both statements true?

> 200   100 <

Practise

1 Order the numbers in each cloud from smallest to largest.

a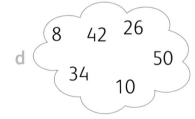
    32
  23   34
    43 54
    45

b
  26
24 28 82
  42
    62

c
  36
34   38
      83
43 63

d
8 42 26
    50
34
  10

e
55 46
19
  28 82
73   37 91
  64

f
  123
154 143 134
  145 132

g
431 791 671
    551
201 311

h
410 542
434
  526 450
  508

i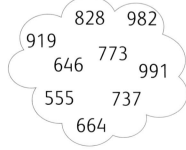
  828 982
919
  646 773
    991
555 737
  664

2 Arrange the digit cards to make number sentences. The first one has been done for you.

a

b  ☐☐ < ☐☐

c

d

e  ☐☐ > ☐☐ > ☐☐

f

g

h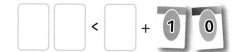

Try this

Copy and insert the correct symbol. Use <, > or =.

Double 24 ☐ 3 × 10   Half 70 ☐ 3 × 10

Double 48 ☐ 9 × 10   Double 35 ☐ 10 × 7

Rounding to the nearest 10 or 100

Learn

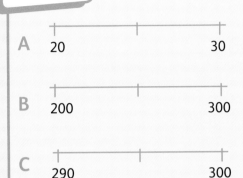

A 20 — 30
B 200 — 300
C 290 — 300

In each case:
- Say the number that is in the middle of the number line.
- Say a number that is to the right of the middle.
- Say a number that is to the left of the middle.

What is 29 rounded to the nearest 10?
What is 291 rounded to the nearest 100?
What is 291 rounded to the nearest 10?

Practise

1 What number is in the middle?

a 30 — 40   b 90 — 100

c 300 — 400   d 350 — 360

2 Copy these number lines. Write two numbers that go in the blue section, and two numbers that go in the yellow section, as shown in a.

a
21 23   26 27
20   30

b 420   430

c 600   700

d 690   700

e 900   1 000

f 990   1 000

3 Round to the nearest 10.

a 39   b 41

c 92   d 99

e 351   f 357

g 456   h 454

Try this

Round to the nearest 10 and to the nearest 100.

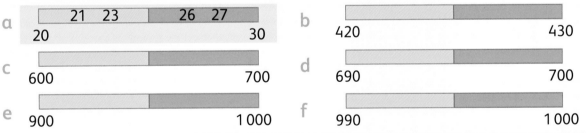

a 281   428   523
b 619   694   698
c 951   991   999

119

Number patterns

(?) (92) [?] [100] (?) (108) [112] [116] (120) (?)

What are the missing numbers?
Continue the pattern. What number is in the sixth circle?

Practise

1 Copy and complete.

a
12   15   18

b
112   115   118

c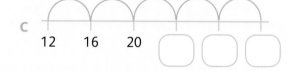
12   16   20

d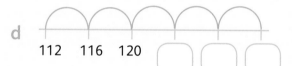
112   116   120

e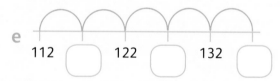
112   122   132

f
        112   312   512

2 What numbers should replace the letters?

40	36	32	A	B	C
42	38	34	D	E	F
142	133	124	G	H	I
242	J	260	K	278	L
M	N	45	54	O	P
145	Q	R	S	T	160

Try this

Design your own number pattern.
Hide half of your numbers under counters. Challenge your partner to guess the hidden numbers.

120

⏻ 11b Fractions

Explore

What will you see when the paper is unfolded?

How many parts will there be?

Try it for yourself and see if your prediction was right.

Now predict what will happen if the folded paper is folded again, and again, and again.

Try it for yourself.

Key words

fraction

numerator

denominator

part

whole

half

third

quarter

Fractions of shapes

Learn

What is the same and what is different about these shapes?

What fraction of each shape is shaded?

This shape is split into three parts.
Two of those parts are shaded.
Jo says $\frac{2}{3}$ of the triangle is shaded.
Explain why Jo is not right.

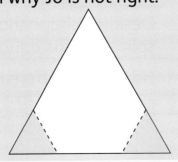

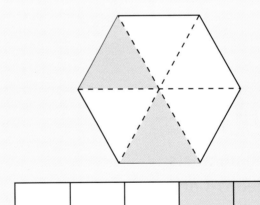

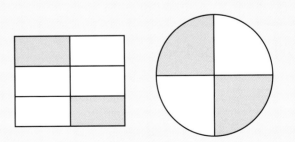

Practise

1 What fraction is shaded?

a    b    c

d   e   f 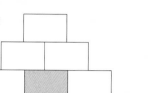   g

h 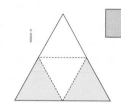   i   j

2 Copy and shade.

a   Shade $\frac{1}{4}$ b   Shade $\frac{1}{10}$

c   Shade $\frac{3}{4}$ d   Shade $\frac{4}{10}$

Learn

Mixed numbers

$1\frac{1}{2}$ means 1 and $\frac{1}{2}$. It is here.

What about $1\frac{1}{4}$?

Try this

Design a shape that is split into nine equal parts.

How many different ways can you shade $\frac{8}{9}$?

Equivalent fractions

Learn

Write the fraction of each shape that is shaded.
What do you notice about the numerator and the denominator?

$\frac{2}{2}$

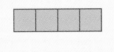

In each of these shapes, one half is shaded.
Write the fraction for each.
What do you notice about the numerators
and denominators?

Practise

1 Write the fraction that is equivalent to one whole.

a b c d 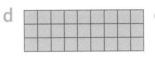 e 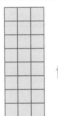 f g

2 Copy these shapes and shade half of each one.
Write the fraction that is equivalent to $\frac{1}{2}$.

a b c d 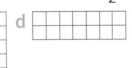 e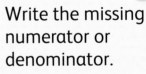

$\frac{3}{6} = \frac{1}{2}$

f g  h 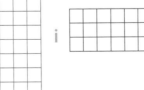 i

Try this

Write the missing
numerator or
denominator.

$\frac{\square}{10} = \frac{1}{2}$ $\frac{10}{\square} = \frac{1}{2}$

$\frac{\square}{20} = \frac{1}{2}$ $\frac{20}{\square} = \frac{1}{2}$

$\frac{\square}{80} = \frac{1}{2}$ $\frac{80}{\square} = \frac{1}{2}$

$\frac{\square}{100} = \frac{1}{2}$ $\frac{100}{\square} = \frac{1}{2}$

11c Fractions of amounts

Explore

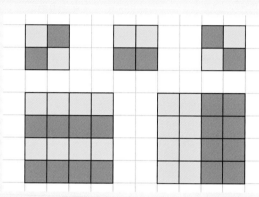

What is the same and what is different about these five diagrams?

What fraction is shaded in each diagram?

What makes these shapes more difficult to shade in half?

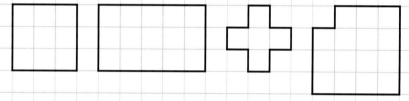

Fractions and division

Learn

There are 20 fish in a tank.

Felix has $\frac{1}{2}$ the fish. Irina has $\frac{1}{4}$ of the fish.

You can find $\frac{1}{4}$ by splitting the group in half, and then finding half again.

I have 15 pet fish. $\frac{1}{3}$ of them are clownfish.

I have 20 pet fish. $\frac{1}{4}$ of them are clownfish.

Who has the most clownfish?

Practise

1 Find these.

 a $\frac{1}{3}$ of 18 cubes   b $\frac{1}{4}$ of 20 cubes   c $\frac{1}{3}$ of 15 cubes   d $\frac{1}{10}$ of 20 cubes

 e $\frac{1}{2}$ of 20 cubes   f $\frac{1}{4}$ of 12 cubes   g $\frac{1}{3}$ of 21 cubes

2 Match each of these to a division calculation and an answer.

 a $\frac{1}{4}$ of 24   e $\frac{1}{10}$ of 50

 b $\frac{1}{3}$ of 24   f $\frac{1}{2}$ of 20

 c $\frac{1}{3}$ of 30   g $\frac{1}{2}$ of 10

 d $\frac{1}{3}$ of 27   h $\frac{1}{10}$ of 10

 $27 \div 3$ $50 \div 10$ $24 \div 4$ $20 \div 2$ $10 \div 10$ $24 \div 3$ $10 \div 2$ $30 \div 3$

 5 8 9 10 1 6 5 10

3 Work out who has the most.

 a Jamil has 40 stickers: $\frac{1}{2}$ are of animals.

   Sharon has 40 stickers: $\frac{1}{10}$ are of animals.

 b Tess has 20 sweets: $\frac{1}{4}$ are orange.

   Joe has 20 sweets: $\frac{1}{2}$ are orange.

 c Lee has 50 fish: $\frac{1}{10}$ are clownfish.

   Lisa has 40 fish: $\frac{1}{10}$ are clownfish.

 d Pedro has 50 fish: $\frac{1}{2}$ are zebra fish, and the rest are clownfish.

   Maria has 40 fish: $\frac{1}{4}$ are zebra fish and the rest are clownfish.

Halving odd and even numbers

Learn

Sandra wants to shade half of this grid.
There are 15 squares.

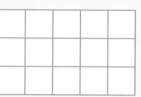

If it was a 14-square grid, she would shade 7, because 7 + 7 = 14.

If it was a 16-square grid, she would shade 8, because 8 × 2 = 16.

What should she shade for this 15-square grid?

Half of 15 is written as $7\frac{1}{2}$.

Practise

1 Copy each shape and shade half.

Write a number sentence to show how many boxes you have shaded in each shape. The first one has been done for you.

a   b   c   d

$$9 \div 2 = 4\frac{1}{2}$$

e

f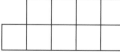

g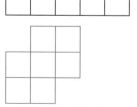

Think like a mathematician

In any fraction question, you can use cubes or counters for the whole amount. Then you can split them into the fractions you need. This will help you to see the link with division.

2 Answer these.

a Half of 20 = ◯
b Half of 21 = ◯
c Half of 30 = ◯
d Half of 31 = ◯
e Half of 50 = ◯
f Half of 25 = ◯
g Half of ◯ = 10
h Half of ◯ = $9\frac{1}{2}$
i Half of ◯ = 20
j Half of ◯ = $19\frac{1}{2}$
k Half of ◯ = 17
l Half of ◯ = $17\frac{1}{2}$

3 Measure and cut out strips of paper to exactly these lengths.

a 12 cm   b 13 cm   c 17 cm   d 18 cm

e 22 cm   f 25 cm   g 29 cm   h 30 cm

Calculate how long half of each strip should be.

Fold each strip in half.

Now measure each half to see if its length matches the calculation.

Stick the strips in your book or make a poster to display in the class.

Label them with the measurements to include $\frac{1}{2}$ cm.

Try this

I am thinking of a number. I double it and add 1. My answer is 33. What number did I start with?

I am thinking of a number. I add 1, then double the answer. My answer is 32. What number did I start with?

Make up some of your own 'I am thinking of a number' problems.

Self-check

A Number and place value

1   Write these numbers from smallest to largest.

916   26   696   206   161   626   906   62   216

2   What is 483 rounded to the nearest 10 and 100?

3   What are the missing numbers?

Continue the pattern. What number is in the third square?

(?) (127) [?] [327] (?) (527)

B Fractions

1   What fraction of this shape is shaded?

2   Copy this shape. Shade half of the shape. Write the fraction that is equivalent to $\frac{1}{2}$.

3   What are the missing whole numbers and fractions on this number line?

[?] [$4\frac{1}{4}$] [?] [?] [5]

C Fractions of amounts

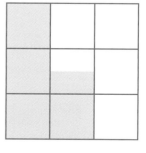

1   Half of this grid is shaded. Write the fraction.

2   What is a $\frac{1}{3}$ of 30 cubes? Write the number.

3   Which division calculation shows $\frac{1}{5}$ of 20?

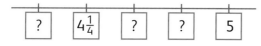

20 ÷ 5   10 ÷ 2   20 ÷ 4   10 ÷ 5   20 ÷ 10

Unit 12   Geometry and problem solving

12a 2-D shapes

Explore

Key words

symmetrical
mirror line
right angle

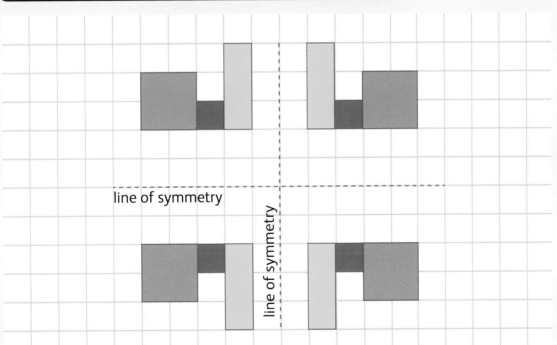

line of symmetry

line of symmetry

What is the same and what is different about the photograph and the diagram?

How many lines of symmetry can you see?

Symmetry

Learn

This shape has at least two mirror lines.

Can you find any more?

How many mirror lines do you think there are altogether?

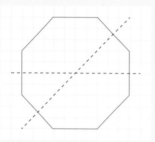

Try this

Make a pattern out of four counters or cubes.

Challenge your partner to add four more counters or cubes to make a symmetrical pattern.

Practise

1 List the shapes that have correct mirror lines marked.

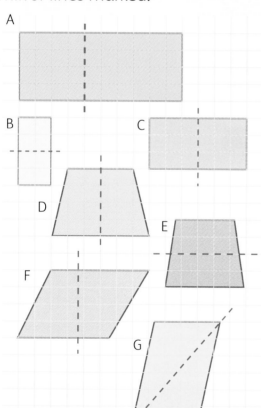

2 Sort the shapes. Copy and complete the table.

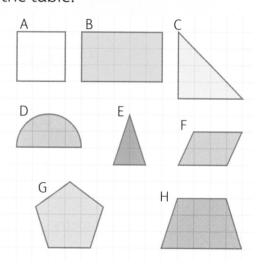

No symmetry	One mirror line	Two mirror lines	More than two mirror lines

Sorting 2-D shapes

Learn

Which shapes are in the right place?

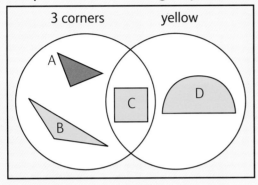

Try this

Draw a Venn diagram.
Choose two labels for your circles from the list below.

- Regular
- Quadrilateral
- Symmetrical
- Odd number of corners
- Even number of edges
- One right angle

Practise

1 a List the shapes that are in the right place.

 b List the shapes that are in the wrong place.

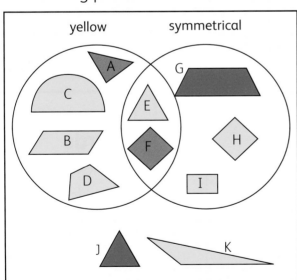

2 Write the names of two shapes for each section.

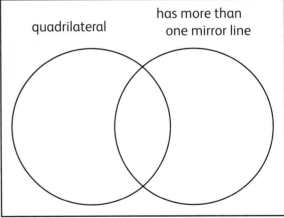

⟳ 12b **Position and movement**

Explore

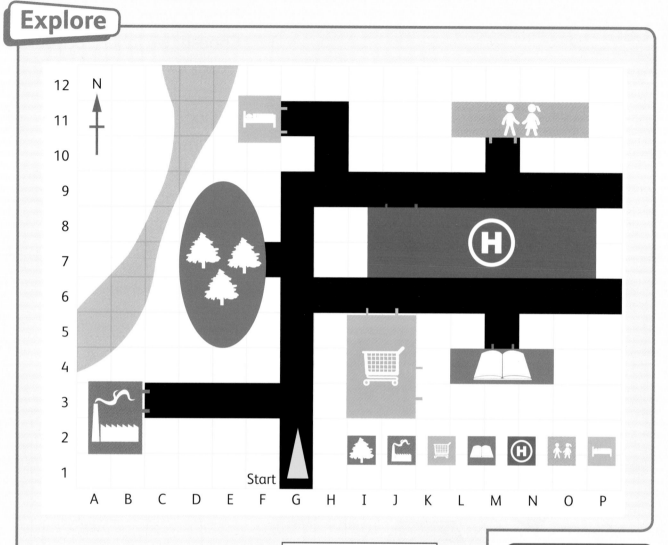

Key

🌲	Forest
🏭	Factory
🛒	Supermarket
📖	Library
Ⓗ	Hospital
👫	School
🛏	Hotel
⊔	Entrance/Exit

Describe how to go from the start to each different place.

How many turns do you have to make to get from the library to the school?

What is at E6?

Key words ⟳

clockwise
anti-clockwise
position
turn
angle
right angle
acute
obtuse

Sorting 2-D shapes

Learn

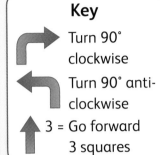

Key

↱ Turn 90° clockwise

↰ Turn 90° anti-clockwise

↑ 3 = Go forward 3 squares

Follow the instructions to see where the car ends up. ↑8 ↰ ↑4

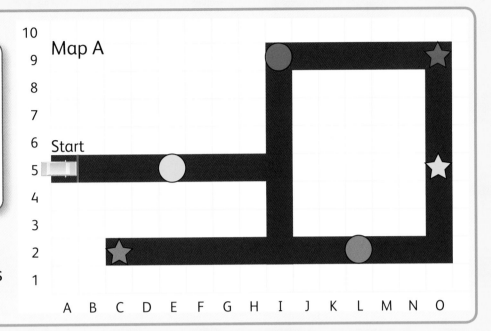

Map A

Practise

1 Write the grid reference for each shape on Map A. One has been done for you.

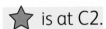 is at C2.

2 Use the key to write instructions to reach each shape in Map A. Return to the start position each time.

3 Write instructions for two different routes to reach the red star in Map A.

4 Use Map B. Write instructions to get from the start and back, collecting each shape along the way.

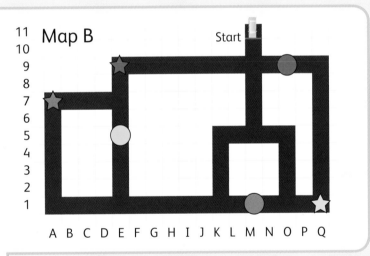

Map B

Try this

Invent your own map. It should have a start position and six shapes. Try to have different routes to get to the same shape.

Challenge your class to write instructions to collect all the shapes.

Right angles

Learn

How many right angles are there?

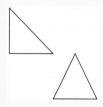

You can use a set-square to check for right angles.

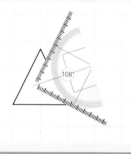

Practise

1 Sort the shapes. Copy and complete the table with the letters of the shapes. The first one has been done for you

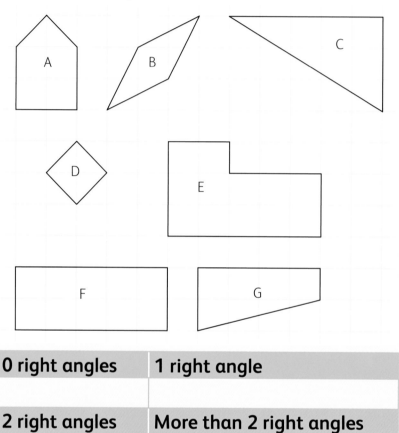

0 right angles	1 right angle
2 right angles	**More than 2 right angles**
Shape G	

Try this

Look at the hands on a clock face. Write four times when the hands form a right angle.

Think like a mathematician

Remember: right angles can be tilted.

Acute and obtuse angles

Learn

Not all angles are right angles.

Angles that are smaller than a right angle are called acute.

Angles that are bigger than a right angle are called obtuse.

Try this

Draw these.

a A triangle with three acute angles.

b A quadrilateral with two obtuse angles.

c A pentagon with an acute angle.

d A hexagon with three acute angles.

e A shape with two right angles, one acute angle and one obtuse angle.

Practise

1 How many acute and obtuse angles are there?

Use a set-square to check.

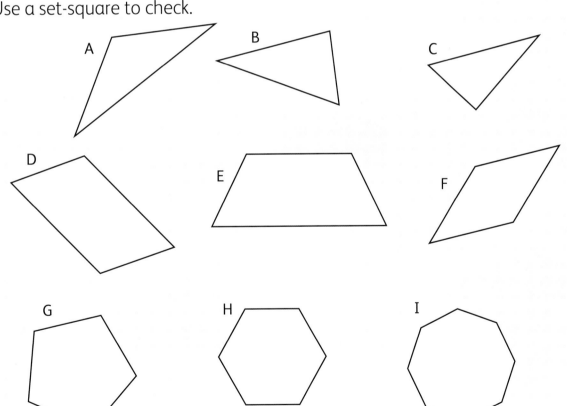

⟳ 12c 3-D shapes

Explore

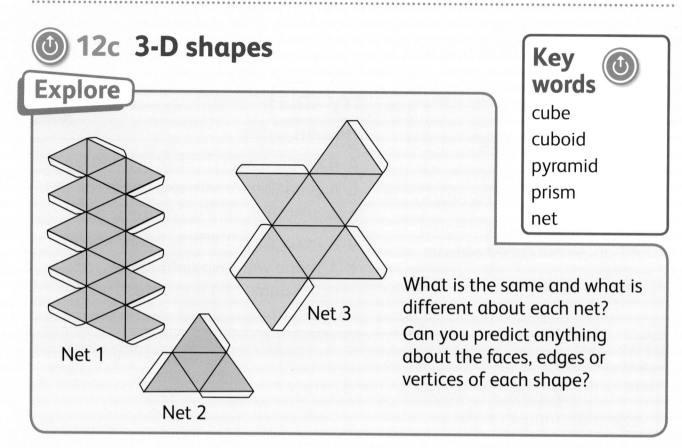

Net 1

Net 2

Net 3

What is the same and what is different about each net?

Can you predict anything about the faces, edges or vertices of each shape?

3-D shapes from cubes

Learn

How many small cubes make this cuboid?

There are different ways to think about it.

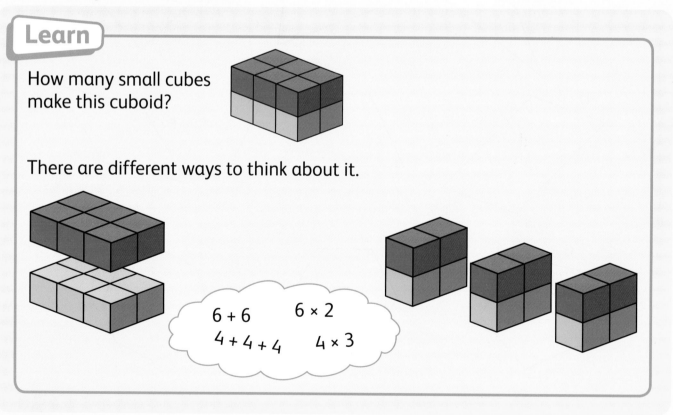

6 + 6   6 × 2

4 + 4 + 4   4 × 3

Practise

1 How many cubes are there in each cuboid?

Write the calculation that you use to work it out. The first one has been done for you.

Make the shapes, and see if you were correct.

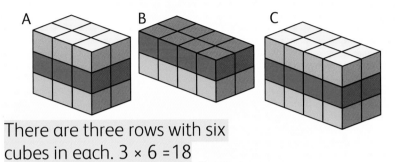

A B C

There are three rows with six cubes in each. 3 × 6 = 18

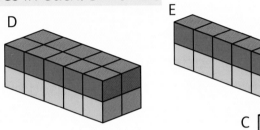

D E

2 How many cubes make each pyramid?

Write the calculation, and check by building the shape.

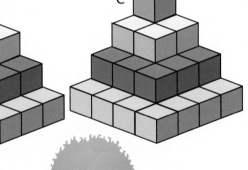

A B C

Predict how many cubes you need to make the next (bigger) pyramid. And then the next one after that.

Try this

One of these shapes is made from four cubes. Which one?

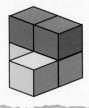

Use four cubes.
Can you make more than seven different shapes? If you can, try to draw them.

Pyramids and prisms

Look at these pyramids.

What is the same and what is different about them?

Say a sentence for each one, using the words vertices, faces or edges.

What would the net for a pentagon-based pyramid look like?

Practise

1 How many faces does each pyramid have?

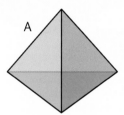 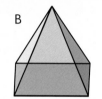

A B

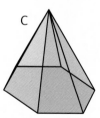 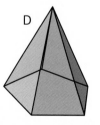

C D

2 These are the bases for four different pyramids. Sketch a net for each.

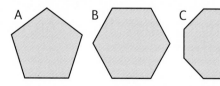

A B C

Try this

Look at these pyramid bases.

Write the number of triangular faces you would need for each shape to turn it into a pyramid.

Now write the number of vertices for each pyramid.

Write the number of edges.

What do you notice?

Self-check

A 2-D shapes

1 Draw a shape that has two mirror lines of symmetry.

2 Copy the table. Sort each shape under the correct heading.

A   B   C

Symmetrical	Even number of vertices	One right angle

3 What is the same and what is different about these two shapes?

B Position and movement

1 Write instructions for two different routes to follow from the red star to the blue circle.

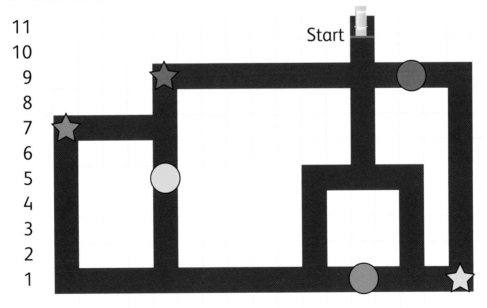

2 a Does this shape have more or less than one right angle? Use a set square to check.

b Is the angle at the top of the shape smaller than, bigger than or equal to a right angle?

C 3-D shapes

1 Draw the 2-D faces for these 3-D shapes.

A B C

2 What is the same and what is different about shape B and shape C?

3 Copy and complete this table for shapes A, B and C.

Number of faces	Number of vertices	Number of edges

Unit 13 Number and problem solving

⟳ 13a Mental strategies

Explore

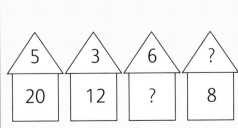

What is the same and what is different about the pictures in each row?

What calculations could represent each picture?

Key words ⟳

double
half
multiply
divide
array

Learn

What are the missing numbers?

To solve this puzzle, look for a pattern in the numbers.

5	3	6	?
20	12	?	8

What if you multiply the number in the roof by four?

Practise

1 Draw a row of houses for the 4× table.

   Start like this.

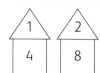

For question 2, work out the rule in each row. Do you have to multiply or divide?

2 Write the missing numbers for the letters A–X.

a
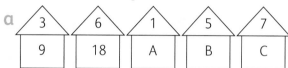

3	6	1	5	7
9	18	A	B	C

b
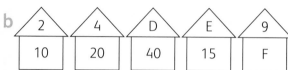

2	4	D	E	9
10	20	40	15	F

c
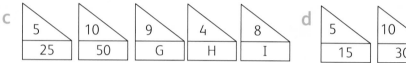

5	10	9	4	8
25	50	G	H	I

d
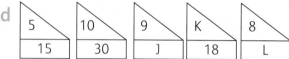

5	10	9	K	8
15	30	J	18	L

e

2	3	8	9	11
4	6	M	N	O

f

2	3	P	8	R
20	30	60	Q	100

g

5	3	1	7	0
50	30	S	T	U

h

5	3	V	W	X
20	12	24	28	32

Try this

Draw four rows of houses. Follow these rules.

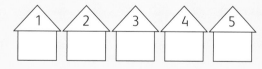

Row 1: Add one to the number in the roof, then multiply the answer by 10.

Row 2: Multiply the number in the roof by 10, then add 1.

Row 3: Add one to the number in the roof, then multiply the answer by 5.

Row 4: Multiply the number in the roof by 5, then add 1.

Doubles and halves

Learn

What do these diagrams show?

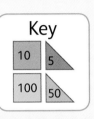

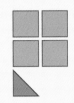 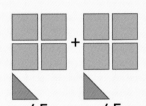 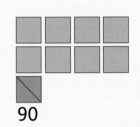

45 + 45 = 90

Practise

1 Double each number shown below. Write a calculation for each.

a  b  c   d

e   f   g  h

i   j   k  l

m   n  o   p

2 Each number has already been doubled.
Work out what the starting number was.

a  b

c   d

e  f

g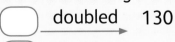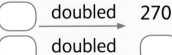

Try this

Find the starting numbers.

◯ ⟶ doubled 130

◯ ⟶ doubled 270

◯ ⟶ doubled ◯ ⟶ doubled 980

Thinking about multiples

Learn

Which numbers go in sections
A, B and C?

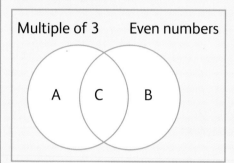

Multiple of 3   Even numbers

21   18
12   30
3   9   5

I cannot see
where to put
number 5.

Practise

1 Sort the numbers from the cloud
   into A, B and C.

   Watch out for numbers that do not
   fit in any section.

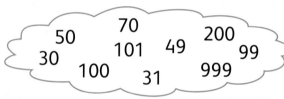

50   70   200
30   101   49   99
100   31   999

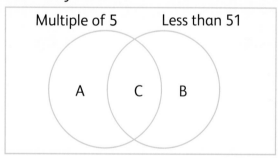

Multiple of 5   Less than 51

2 Sort the numbers from the cloud
   into A, B and C.

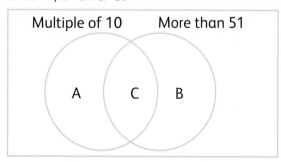

Multiple of 10   More than 51

Try this

Write at least one number that
would go in each section.

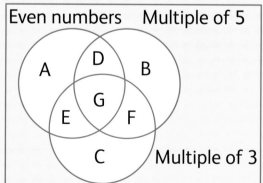

Even numbers   Multiple of 5

A   D   B
G
E   F
C   Multiple of 3

⟲ 13b Addition and subtraction

Explore

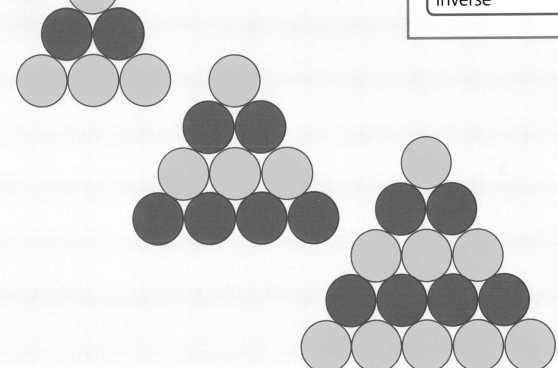

This is a growing pattern.

What calculations can you use to work out how many circles there are in each pattern?

How many circles would you need to draw the next pattern? And the next? And even the next?

Complements to 100

Learn

How are these three calculations linked?

Do you have to start every question from the beginning?

60 + ⬭ = 100   65 + ⬭ = 100   66 + ⬭ = 100

```
      +?                           +?
   ╭────────────╮              ╭────────╮
  60         100         +?
                      ╭──╮
                     65        100
```

Practise

1 Draw number lines to solve these. The first one has been done for you.

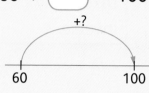

   a 30 + 70 = 100   +70   35 + ☐ = 100   36 + ☐ = 100

   b 80 + ☐ = 100   30 40 50 60 70 80 90 100   85 + ☐ = 100   89 + ☐ = 100

2 Solve.

   a ☐ + 20 = 100   b ☐ + 40 = 100   c ☐ + 90 = 100

      ☐ + 18 = 100   ☐ + 37 = 100   ☐ + 86 = 100

   d 100 − ☐ = 20   e 100 − ☐ = 30   f 100 − ☐ = 60

      100 − ☐ = 25   100 − ☐ = 32   100 − ☐ = 66

3 Six athletes are running in a 100 m race.
How far does each athlete still have to run?

Runner 1 has run 56 m.

Runner 2 has run 10 more metres than runner 1.

Runner 3 is 4 m behind runner 2.

Runner 4 has run half as far as runner 3.

Runner 5 is 23 m past the halfway point.

Runner 6 is 11 m ahead of runner 5.

Try this

Use two 1–6 spinners. Spin both spinners to make a two-digit number. Write the number that must be added to your two-digit number to make 100. Repeat five times.

Adding and subtracting mentally

Learn

12 − 5 = 7

Once you know this fact, you can do these subtractions mentally.

| 32 − 5 | 132 − 5 | 142 − 5 |
| 342 − 5 | 772 − 5 | 992 − 5 |

What about 102 − 5?

Practise

13 − 5 = 8   14 − 5 = 9   9 + 2 = 11   8 + 3 = 11   7 + 4 = 11

1 What patterns do you see in these calculations? Use the subtraction pattern to help you answer these.

a	b	c	d
23 − 5	273 − 5	34 − 5	284 − 5
43 − 5	363 − 5	54 − 5	354 − 5
93 − 5	873 − 5	84 − 5	884 − 5
133 − 5	993 − 5	254 − 5	994 − 5

2 Use the subtraction or addition pattern to help you answer these.

a ☐ + 2 = 21   b ☐ + 2 = 41

c ☐ + 2 = 141   d ☐ + 2 = 351

e ☐ + 3 = 21   f ☐ + 3 = 41

g ☐ + 3 = 141   h ☐ + 3 = 351

i ☐ + 4 = 31   j ☐ + 4 = 51

k ☐ + 4 = 151   l ☐ + 4 = 361

m 181 − ☐ = 178   n 151 − ☐ = 147

o 239 = 241 − ☐   p 378 = 381 − ☐

Try this

Find the missing numbers:

☐ + 8 = 233

☐ − 8 = 233

237 = ☐ − 9

237 = ☐ + 9

245 − ☐ = 238

238 + ☐ = 245

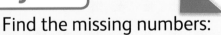

Adding by writing notes

Learn

When I cannot work out an addition in my head, I make notes to help. Look at 42 + 23. I would start with 42, add 20, then add 3.

42 + 20 = 62

62 + 3 = 65

So 42 + 23 = 65.

Practise

Razik is 112 cm tall. How high off the ground is he if he stands on each box?

Ellie is 119 cm tall. How high off the ground is she if she stands on each box?

A 23 cm   B 35 cm   C 41 cm

D 57 cm   E 62 cm   F 74 cm

2 Answer these. Write notes to help you.

a 45 + 32
   45 + 42
   45 + 52

b 45 + 33
   45 + 43
   45 + 53

c 145 + 34
   245 + 44
   345 + 54

d 88 + 25
   88 + 35
   88 + 45

e 188 + 25
   188 + 35
   188 + 45

f 188 + 26
   189 + 26
   189 + 27

3 Find the missing digits.

| ? | 4 | + | 4 | ? | = 85 |

| ? | 4 | + | 4 | ? | = 95 |

| 5 | ? | + | ? | 4 | = 105 |

| 8 | ? | + | ? | 5 | = 121 |

| ? | 7 | + | 4 | ? | = 135 |

| 5 | ? | + | ? | 4 | = 134 |

Try this

Place these digits in the grid. How many different totals can you get?

2 4 + 6 8

? ? + ? ?

Subtracting by writing notes

Learn

When I cannot work out a subtraction in my head, I make notes to help. Look at 42 – 23. I would start with 42, take away 20, then take away 3

$$42 - 20 = 22$$
$$22 - 3 = 19$$

So 42 – 23 = 19.

Practise

1

Coach A seats 17 people.	Coach D seats 48 people.
Coach B seats 22 people.	Coach E seats 55 people.
Coach C seats 35 people.	Coach F seats 63 people.

There are 250 people at a show.
First, coach A takes 17 people away.
Then coach B takes 22 people away.
The rest of the coaches leave in order.
Work out how many people are left after each coach leaves.

2 Answer these.

a 45 – 32   b 45 – 33   c 145 – 36
   45 – 42   45 – 43   245 – 46
                            345 – 56

d 88 – 25   e 188 – 25   f 188 – 29
   88 – 35   188 – 35   189 – 28
   88 – 45   188 – 45   189 – 27

3 (120) –1→ (119) –2→ (117) –3→ …

Start on 120.

Take away 1.

Then take away 2 from the answer.

Then take away 3 from that answer.

Keep going by taking away 4, then 5, then 6 …

What number do you take away to reach 0?

Now try starting on 210.

13c **Multiplication and division**

Explore

Key words
multiply
divide
times tables
multiple
array

How many players can play a game using these cards so that everyone has a fair share?

What about now?

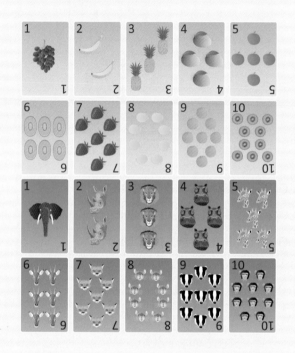

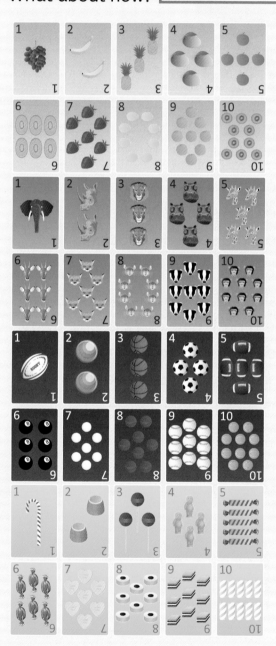

Investigate with 17 cards.

Is there always a remainder when we share these cards? Explain how you know.

Linking multiplication and division

Learn

Write a multiplication and a division statement to go with this diagram.

15		
5	5	5

I can see that 3 times 5 = 15.

I can see that 15 divided by 3 = 5.

Practise

1 Write a multiplication and a division statement for these.

a
30				
6	6	6	6	6

b
30					
5	5	5	5	5	5

c
28			
7	7	7	7

d
24		
8	8	8

e
18								
2	2	2	2	2	2	2	2	2

f
10				
2	2	2	2	2

2 Write **two** multiplications and **two** divisions to go with each array.

a b c

d  e

f 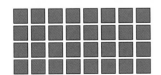 g

Try this

 + = 50

5 × 6   4 × 5

Do these calculations.
Add the answers.
The total is 50.
Draw 5 different pairs of arrays that add up to 50.

Multiplying two-digit numbers

Learn

What happens if you join these arrays?

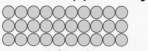

    10 × 3   3 × 3

This tells you how to work out 13 × 3.

    10 × 3   3 × 3

13 × 3 = 30   +   9
          10 × 3 + 3 × 3

What calculation does this show?

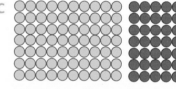

    10 × 4   2 × 4

Practise

1 Write the calculation to go with each diagram.

a

b

c

d

e

f

g

h

2 Draw arrays for these.

a 11 × 4

10 × 4 = 40
1 × 4 = 4
11 × 4 = 40 + 4 = 44

b 13 × 4   c 15 × 4   d 17 × 4
e 15 × 5   f 15 × 4   g 15 × 3

Write the answer to each calculation.

3

Activity price list	
Swimming	$5
Tennis	$4
Dance workshop	$3
Gymnastics	$4
Art	$5

30 learners take part in an activity day.
Work out the cost.

a 12 choose swimming, 18 choose dance

b 18 choose swimming, 12 choose dance

c 11 choose tennis, 19 choose swimming

d 19 choose tennis, 11 choose swimming

4
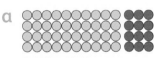

36 ÷ 3 = 12
12 × 3 = 36.

I know 12 × 3 = 36.
I can also find divisions like
36 ÷ 3 by using the inverse.

Write the answer to each division.

a

52 ÷ 4

b

39 ÷ 3

c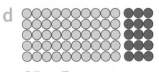

45 ÷ 3

d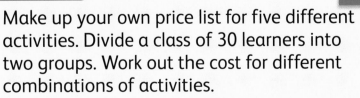

65 ÷ 5

Try this

Make up your own price list for five different activities. Divide a class of 30 learners into two groups. Work out the cost for different combinations of activities.

What is the closest total you can get to $100?

153

Patterns and rules

Learn

Look at this number trail.

If you start with 5, you get 11 as the final answer.

Practise

1 Solve these number trails. Look for patterns.

a 1 ×5 +5

b 3 ×5 +5

c 5 ×5 +5

d 1 ×5 −1

e 3 ×5 −1

f 5 ×5 −1

g 2 ×5 +4

h 4 ×5 +4

i 6 ×5 +4

2 Predict how these patterns will continue.
Will you ever get an answer of 100 for any of them? How do you know?

a	b	c	d	e
1 × 10 + 5	1 × 10 + 10	1 × 10 + 1	1 × 10 − 1	1 × 5 + 5
2 × 10 + 5	2 × 10 + 10	2 × 10 + 2	2 × 10 − 2	2 × 5 + 10
3 × 10 + 5	3 × 10 + 10	3 × 10 + 3	3 × 10 − 3	3 × 5 + 5
4 × 10 + 5	4 × 10 + 10	4 × 10 + 4	4 × 10 − 4	4 × 5 + 10

3 Try different starting numbers for these number trails.
Can you get an answer of exactly 50?

a ×2 +1

b ×2 +2

c ×5 +20

d ×5 −20

e ×5 ×2

f ×2 ×5

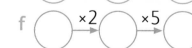

Self-check

A Mental strategies

1 Use the 4× table to work out the missing numbers.

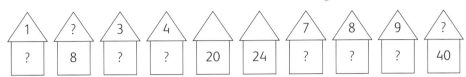

2 Use the key to work out the total for this diagram.

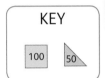

KEY

100   50

3 I think of a number. I double it, then double the answer.
My final answer is 700. What number did I start with?

B Addition and subtraction

1 Write the missing numbers.

a $\boxed{} + 6 = 421$ b $\boxed{} - 6 = 421$

2 Write notes to solve these calculations.

a $234 + 45 = \boxed{}$ b $187 - 17 = \boxed{}$

3 Solve the number trail. What do you notice about the last number?

(92) +1 ◯ +2 ◯ +3 ◯ −1 ◯ −2 ◯ −3 ◯

C Multiplication and division

1 Write a multiplication and a division statement for these.

a

15				
3	3	3	3	3

b

35				
7	7	7	7	7

2 Write a multiplication and a division
to go with this array.

3 Which of these number trails has an answer of 50?

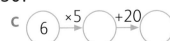

a (10) ×2 ◯ +1 ◯   b (25) ×2 ◯ +2 ◯   c (6) ×5 ◯ +20 ◯

 14a Money

Explore

The prices have been removed. Make reasonable estimates. Use these as the actual prices.

Look at this shop. How many different things can you buy here?

What could you buy for $1?
What could you buy for about $5?
Invent a shopping list for $10.

Key words

dollar
cent
amount
cost
change
add
subtract

Money and halving

Learn

Our grandmother gave us $5 to share equally.

I wonder how we would share $5 equally? We would still get two $1 notes each but there would be a $1 note left over.

Try this

How much would it cost if you got a full clean every month for a year?

What if you also got your tyres checked?

Practise

1 Biren and Tessa made money from a cake sale each week. Work out how much each learner got if they shared the money equally.

Week 1 $6
Week 2 $7
Week 3 $10
Week 4 $9
Week 5 $13
Week 6 $17
Week 7 $18
Week 8 $11

2

Clean car services	
Full clean	$11
Wax	$4
Polish	$5
Tyre check	$8
Oil change	$12
Screen wash	$7

Work out the cost of these services.

a Full clean and tyre check

b Wax and polish

c Oil change and screen wash

d Full clean and wax

e Oil change, wax and polish

f Wax, polish and tyre check.

There is a half-price sale on Saturday. Work out the new cost of the services in a–f.

Writing money with $ and c

Learn

What would the diagram look like for:

Is there another way to write 150c?

How many cents in $2.50?

Practise

1 Convert to $ and cents.

a 150c = $⬚ and ⬚c b 250c = $⬚ and ⬚c c 350c = $⬚ and ⬚c
  151c = $⬚ and ⬚c   251c = $⬚ and ⬚c   450c = $⬚ and ⬚c
  152c = $⬚ and ⬚c   252c = $⬚ and ⬚c   550c = $⬚ and ⬚c

2 How many cents are there in each amount?

a ⬚c = $1.10   b ⬚c = $1.01   c ⬚c = $2.10
  ⬚c = $1.11   ⬚c = $1.02   ⬚c = $2.01
  ⬚c = $1.12   ⬚c = $1.03   ⬚c = $2.20

3 Order from smallest to largest.

a 21c	12c	221c	120c	210c	121c	201c
b 29c	1c	209c	299c	199c	200c	92c
c $1.20	102c	21c	$1.01	111c	11c	
d $2.02c	220c	$2	$2.22	$2.01	212c	

Money problems

Learn

Fabio's Ice Cream Shop

2 scoops	$1.25
3 scoops	$1.75
4 scoops	$2.10
Chocolate sauce	50c
Sprinkles	60c
Fruit syrup	25c
Toffee stick	99c

How much is 2 scoops with sprinkles?

$1.25 + 60c.

$1.25 ⟶ [$ 1 $] + (25)

Now we can work out:

$1 + 25c + 60c

$1 + 85c = $1.85.

How much is 3 scoops plus chocolate sauce?

$1.75 + 50c

$1 + 75c + 50c

$1 + 125c

Practise

1 Work out the cost from the list above.

  a 2 scoops with chocolate sauce

  b 2 scoops with sprinkles

  c 2 scoops with fruit syrup

  d 3 scoops with sprinkles

2 Work out the cost.

  a 2 scoops plain and 3 scoops plain

  b 2 scoops with sprinkles and 3 scoops plain

  c 2 scoops plain and 3 scoops with sprinkles

  d 2 scoops with chocolate sauce and 3 scoops with sprinkles

3 Solve.

  a $1.99 + ☐ = $2

  b $2.99 + ☐ = $3

  c $3.99 + ☐ = $4

  d $4.99 + ☐ = $5

Try this

With $5, you can buy a number of different ice creams at Fabio's shop.

Work out six different options for ice creams, and show the change you would get from $5.

14b Capacity

Explore

Estimate how many cubes will fit.

Make a container out of your hands, like this.

Estimate how many cubes will fit.

Now ask your partner to add cubes, a few at a time, until no more will fit.

This is one way of measuring capacity. Can you think of more accurate ways?

Key words

measure
capacity
litre
millilitre
scale
division

Reading scales

Learn

What does each line represent?   How much juice is in this jug?

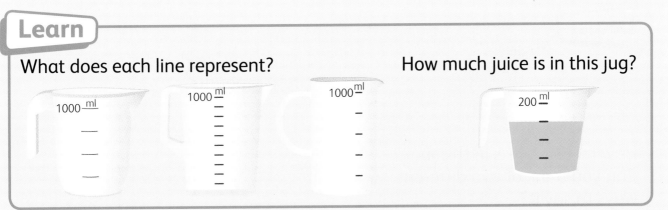

Practise

1 How much is in each jug?

2 How much must be added to fill up each jug?

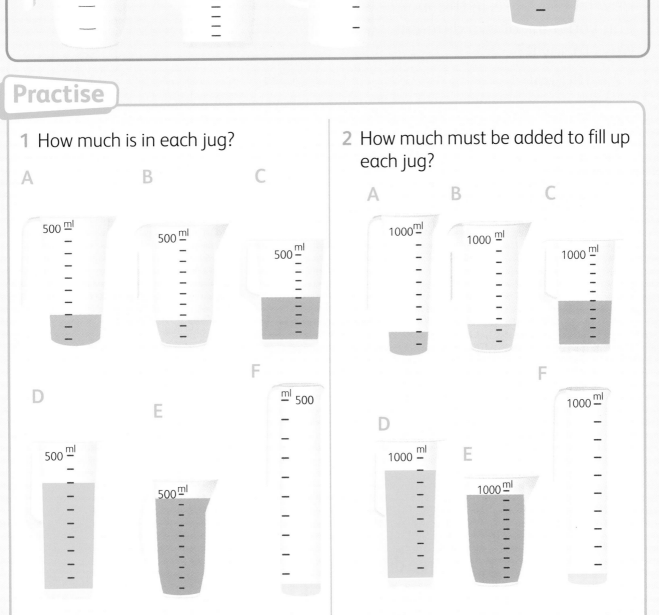

Measuring and estimating in litres and millilitres

2000 ml
1500 —
1000 —
500 —

How much juice is in this jug?
Can you think of two different
ways to say it?

1 ℓ = 1000 ml

List two different ways of writing
these amounts.

2000 ml

2000 ml

2000 ml

1 Estimate how much is in each jug.

1000 ml   2000 ml   200 ml   800 ml   800 ml   1000 ml   1000 ml   200 ml

2 Match the equal measurements. An example has been done for you.

1 ℓ	2 $\frac{1}{2}$ ℓ	$\frac{1}{2}$ ℓ	3 $\frac{1}{4}$ ℓ
$\frac{1}{2}$ ℓ			
1 $\frac{1}{2}$ ℓ	3 $\frac{1}{2}$ ℓ		3 ℓ

2500 ml	2000 ml	3500 ml
3000 ml	1000 ml	
1500 ml	500 ml	3250 ml

Share 1000 ml among three different jugs.

Look very carefully at how much is in each jug, and see
if the numbers add up to 1000 ml exactly. If they do
not, what has happened? Has some water disappeared?

 **Time**

Explore

Sun	Mon	Tues	Weds	Thurs	Fri	Sat
				1	2 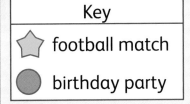	3
4	5	6	7	8	9	10
11	12	13	14	15	16	17
18	19	20	21	22	23	24
25	26	27	28			

Sun	Mon	Tues	Weds	Thurs	Fri	Sat
				1	2	3
4	5	6	7	8	9	10
11	12	13	14	15	16	17
18	19	20	21	22	23	24
25	26	27	28	29	30	31

Key words

second
minute
hour
day
week
month
calendar
digital
analogue

Key	
☆	football match
●	birthday party

Which months do these calendars show?

What is the longest wait between football matches?

How long is it from the first birthday party to the second birthday party? Can you say the answer in two different ways?

How many different mathematical questions can you make up about this calendar?

Digital and analogue clocks

Learn

Find all the
matching
times.

half past 2

2:30

quarter to 3

quarter past 2

2:45

2:15

Practise

1 Match the analogue time to the
digital time. For example:

A matches H 1:30

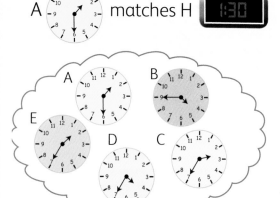

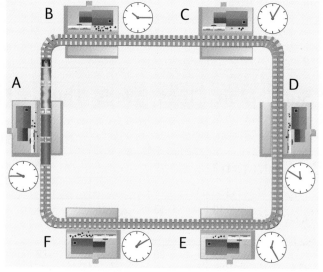

2 a How long does it take from station A
to station B?

b How long does it take from station B
to station D?

c Which is the longest part of the
journey from A back to A?

d How long does the whole journey take?

e What time would you arrive at each
station if the train left half an hour late?

Time problems

Learn

Keep Fit Sports Centre	
Activity timings	
Running session	30 minutes
Football training	1 hour
Swimming lesson	45 minutes
Tennis lesson	1 hour 30 mins
Basketball coaching	2 hours
Gymnastics	70 minutes

If I start a tennis lesson at 10.45, when will it finish?

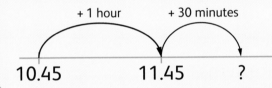

10.45   11.45   ?

Practise

1 Hasan arrives at 11.45. What time will he finish playing basketball and football if he starts at 11.45?

2 What are the finish times for the activities in the table?

TIMETABLE		
Start time	**Activity 1**	**Activity 2**
a 9.15	Football	Tennis
b 10.15	Swimming	Gymnastics
c 10.45	Tennis	Running
d 11.05	Running	Basketball
e 11.45	Basketball	Football
f 12.30	Gymnastics	Swimming

Try this

Design a timetable for a day full of sports training.

Show the start time for each activity.

Include 10 minutes break between each session.

Include 45 minutes for lunch.

Think like a mathematician

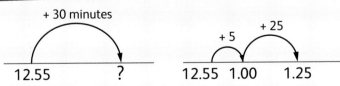

12.55   ?   12.55 1.00   1.25

If you have to add minutes that go over an hour, break the jump into two smaller jumps.

Self-check

A Money

1 Convert to dollars and cents.
   a 110c   b 499c   c 850c   d 305c

2 One tomato costs 15c and a watermelon costs $5. What is the total cost for two tomatoes and one watermelon? How much change will you get if you pay with a $10 note?

3 Make up your own money problem for this calculation.
   $2 + $1.25 + 80c

B Measuring capacity

1 Estimate how many of these jugs you need to fill a 2-litre jug.

   Now measure. Was your estimate correct?

2 Write the ml or ℓ for the amount of juice in these jugs.

   a   b   c

   a ☐ ℓ

   b ☐ ml

   c ☐ ℓ and ☐ ml

3 Pour the juice in these jugs into a 1-litre jug. How many ml are there? How much juice do you need to fill the jug?

C Time

1 The second term of school starts on 22 March and ends on 14 June. How many weeks are there in this term? How many days are there?

2 Write the times shown on these clocks in words.

   a    b

3. The digital clock shows a time in the morning. The analogue clock shows a time in the afternoon. How many hours and minutes are there between these two times?

15a Problem solving

Explore Pattern Street

These are the first ten houses on Pattern Street at night. There are houses on one side of the street only. The houses are numbered in order: 1, 2, 3, and so on. The street has 100 houses. All the sections in this unit are about Pattern Street.

On Pattern Street, every short house is next to a tall house.

The roofs also form a pattern. Can you spot it?

Every fifth house has round windows. All the others have square windows.

If a house has the digit three in its number, then it is painted pink.

Picture problems

1 Describe house number 5 in Pattern Street.

2 What is the same about all the even-numbered houses?

3 What would house number 11 look like?

4 What is the number of the first short house to have a pointy roof?

5 Which of the houses is pink with round windows?

Pattern problems

This is what the first three houses in Pattern Street look like in the daytime. Use the patterns from Explore to solve these problems.

1 Work out what house 6 looks like, without looking at the pictures. Tell your partner how you decided.

2 a What does house 12 look like? Draw it.

b What does house 19 look like? Draw it.

c Is house 20 short or tall? How do you know? What are its windows like?

3 How many pink houses are between these houses?

a House 1 and house 20?

b House 20 and house 50?

c House 1 and house 100?

Logic problems

1 List the houses in Pattern Street that are short with a round roof.

Make a list or a table to help you. Begin it like this.

House 2 and house 8 are in both lists, so they are both tall with round roofs.

Round roof	Tall houses
②	②
5	4
⑧	6
11	⑧
14	10
…	…

2 Consider houses 1 to 50.
List the numbers of houses that are:

  a Short with a round roof

  b Tall with a round roof

  c Short with round windows

  d Tall with a pointy roof

  e Short and pink

  f Tall and pink.

3 A car is parked outside every house with a number in the 9× table.

There is a tree at every house with a 9 in its number.

  a Which houses have a tree and a car outside?

  b Which pink houses have a car?

  c Do any houses with round windows have a tree outside them?

4 One person lives in house 1.
Two people live in house 2.
Three people live in house 3.
This pattern keeps going, so four people live in house 4.

  a How many people live in the first five houses in total?

  b How many people live in the first ten houses in total?

  c Which house has the one hundredth person living in it?

  d If you add up the people living in houses 10 to 15, is the answer more than 100?

  e How many people live in the first five even-numbered houses altogether?

  f How many people live in the first five odd-numbered houses?

  g How many people live in the first three houses with round windows?

  h How many people live in the first five pink houses?

  i Between houses 1 and 100, how many houses are there with round windows and a car in front?

Self-check

A Problem solving

1 There are 30 houses in the next street. If the houses on both sides follow this pattern, what kind of roof would the 12th house have? Show how you worked out the answer.

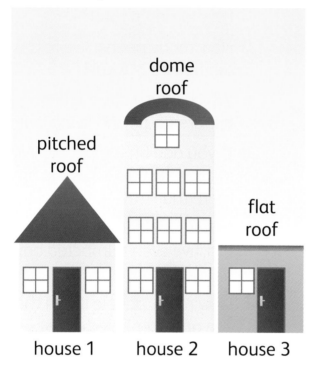

pitched roof

dome roof

flat roof

house 1   house 2   house 3

2 How many houses on both sides of the street would have a rounded roof?

3 Four people live in house 1. Eight people live in house 2. Twelve people live in house 3. How many people live in houses with pitched roofs in this street?
Make a list or a table to help you work out the answer.

Mathematical dictionary

2-digit number a number with a tens digit and a ones digit

2-D shape a flat shape with sides and angles

3-D shape a solid shape with faces, edges and vertices

A

acute an angle that is less than 90 degrees

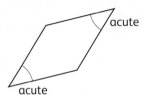

add to find a sum

addition a calculation of the sum of two numbers or things

amount how much

analogue showing time by the hands of a clock or watch

angle the space between when two lines meet

anti-clockwise in the opposite direction to the hands of a clock

array a rectangular arrangement of quantities

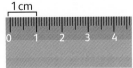

3 × 3

B

bar chart a chart that uses bars to show the relationship between groups of information

Cars in a car park

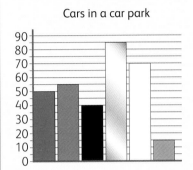

base the lowest part or edge of something such as of a shape

C

calendar a chart showing all the days, weeks and months in a year

capacity the largest amount that something can contain

Carroll diagram a sorting table used to sort items by two or more rules or conditions

cent a coin value

centimetre there are 100 centimetres in one metre

1 cm

change money given back if too much money is given at first

clockwise in the same direction as the hands of a clock

coin a piece of metal used as money

compare to note similarities and differences

corner where two lines meet and form an angle

corner

cost the price of an object

count back continue counting by going down in numbers

count on continue counting by going up in numbers

cube a solid shape with 6 square faces

cuboid a solid shape with 6 rectangular faces

D

data information

day a unit of 24 hours

decrease get smaller

denominator a number below the line in a fraction, the divisor $\longrightarrow \frac{3}{4}$

diagram a drawing to show a problem in visual form

digit symbol for a number

digital show the time with a number rather than the hands of a clock or watch

divide to find how many times a number goes into another number

division separate something into parts

dollar a unit of money

double twice as many

E

edge the side of an object

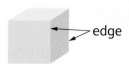

edge

estimate guess

F

face surface of a solid shape

fraction a part of something or part of a number, for example, $\frac{1}{2}$

frequency how often something happens

function the rule that gives the relationship between two numbers or objects

G

gram there are 1000 grams in one kilogram

greater than more than

H

half something divided by 2

half past 30 minutes past the hour

halve to divide by 2

height a unit of measure, how tall a person or object is

hour 60 minutes

hundreds plural for hundred

I

increase get bigger in size or number

input the number, or information that is put into a function

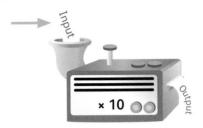

inverse the opposite of an operation, for example, subtraction is the inverse of addition

irregular not usual or normal

J

jottings showing your working out to solve a problem

K

kilogram a measurement of weight, 1000 grams

kilometre a measure of distance, 1000 metres

L

length how far from one point to another

less not as many

less than smaller than in size or number

list a number of items normally written one under the other

litre a measure of volume

M

mass how much an item weighs

measure to find out the size or weight of something there is using a standard tool such as a measuring tape or a measuring scale

method the way to do something

metre a unit of length

millilitre there are 1000 millilitres in one litre

minus take away or subtract

minute there are 60 minutes in one hour

mirror line the line that makes both sides of something the same, so that one side looks as though it has been flipped

money coins or banknotes used to pay for goods and services

month there are 12 months in a year: January, February, March, April, May, June, July, August, September, October, November, December

more greater in number

more than greater in size or number

multiple a number that can be divided equally

multiplication a way of calculating the product of two numbers

multiply to increase in number

N

nearest closest to

net a pattern on paper that you can cut and fold to make a model of a 3-D shape

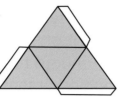

number line a line on which numbers are marked

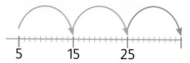

number story a short story that makes it easier to understand a mathematical problem

numerator the number above the line in a fraction that shows how many parts of the whole there are $\longrightarrow \frac{3}{4}$

O

obtuse an angle that is bigger than 90 degrees

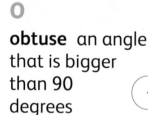
obtuse
obtuse

ones numbers up to 9, show the ones place value

order an arrangement of objects

output the answer or solution

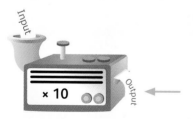

P

part a piece of, or fraction of a whole

partition separate a number into different parts

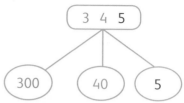

pattern something that repeats regularly, things that are arranged according to a rule

pictogram a picture that represents a word or a number

place value the value every digit has in a number, for example, a one, a hundred or a thousand

100s	10s	1s
	5	3

position place

predict guess how something will happen in the future

prism a solid with two identical ends and flat sides

problem something that needs an answer or solution

properties the qualities or characteristics that a number or object has

puzzle a game or problem

pyramid a solid with triangular sides

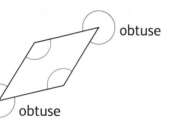

Q

quadrilateral a 2-D shape that has 4 straight sides

quarter something divided by 4

quarter past 15 minutes past the hour

quarter to 15 minutes to the hour

R

rectangle a 2-D shape with two pairs of equal sides

regular usual or normal

remainder something left over

right angle an angle that is exactly 90 degrees

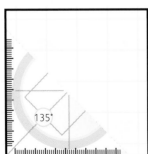

rounding increasing or decreasing a number to the nearest digit (tens, hundreds and so on)

rule the set pattern or laws

S

scale an object that is used to measure weight

second comes after first

side a line of a shape

split divide into pieces or parts

square a 2-D shape with 4 sides of equal length

strategy a method to solve a mathematical problem

subtract to take away something from another

subtraction a way of finding the difference between two numbers or things

sum the total after adding numbers

symmetrical each half is exactly the same

symmetry when a straight line can be drawn through an object or shape to divide it into two parts so that one side looks like a mirror image of the other side

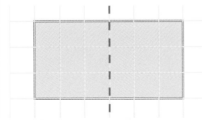

T

table information arranged in rows and columns

take away minus or subtract

tally chart a chart that has a tick, tally or line to show information

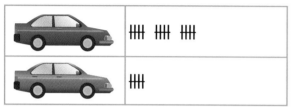

tens the place value that shows a number multiplied by ten

third comes after second

time a measurement of an action or event

times tables a table showing numbers multiplied together

total the answer to an addition calculation

triangle a 2-D shape with 3 sides

triangular an object that is shaped like a triangle

turn to rotate or change position

 Turn 90° clockwise

V

Venn diagram a diagram with circles to show sets

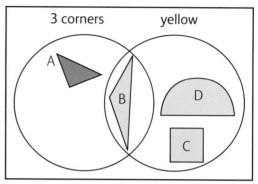

vertex the point where two sides or lines meet

vertices (plural for vertex) the point where two sides or lines meet

W

week there are 7 days in a week: Monday, Tuesday, Wednesday, Thursday, Friday, Saturday, Sunday

weigh find out the weight of an object

weight how much something weighs

whole something that is complete, or in one piece

Y

year 365 (or 366) days make one year